Other books by Torrance Stephens

Novels & Novellas
a matter of attention
last from go

Short Stories
fast and gamin'
butter brown
rock star, stud, gigolo
freak type scene

Essays
dirt behind my ears
brilliant dumb
negro comfortable
nobel neocolonialism: u.s. west asian, north and east african
foreign policy under the obama administration
the legacy of the bush-obama keynesian dialect and income inequality in america: a journal
the rise of establishment politics: essays on U.S. politics during the
bush and obama adminstrations

Poetry
for u who left me while I slept
late nite winds of club paradise
anonymous guest
F0r +h3 B1rds Poems in 140 ch4r4c+3rs 0r l3ss: (For the Birds Poems
in 140 Characters of Less)

Plays
why I'm a ganster and other plays

History
the 3rd republic: nigeria's transition to democracy as told by national print media, 1992-1993

i

RAW DOG BUFFALO PRESS
PALMETTO/MEMPHIS/WHEREVER
© 2017
BY TORRANCE STEPHENS
@RAWDAWGBUFFALO

I Don't Get Down Like That
And other Essays

"News is what someone wants to suppress. Everything else is advertising."
Rubin Frank, Former President NBC news

"Our job is to give people not what they want, but what we decide they ought to have."
Richard Salent, Former President CBS News.

TABLE OF CONTENTS

TABLE OF CONTENTS

TABLE OF CONTENTS

BLM Adopts Jim Crow and Promote Black Codes Policy

On a Sunday morning the 15th of September in 1963, the Ku Klux Klan murdered four girls when they bombed the Sixteenth Street Baptist Church in Birmingham, Alabama. The church, which had been built in 1911, would be the last place Addie Mae Collins, Denise McNair, Carole Robertson, and Cynthia Wesley would ever grace. This was one of the seminal events that propelled the civil rights movement to the forefront of the American consciousness as well shock the nation, presenting it with the horrors blacks in the south and across the U.S. had been dealing with for decades. In basic terms it painted the evil of segregation by race and the incongruence of the premise of separate but equal in the land of the free.

It seems that all of that was struggled for just fifty plus years ago has been thrown down the drain by self-pitying, micro-aggressed, spoiled self-proclaimed social justice warriors whom appear ill-equipped and unable to exist in the real world without artificially constructing it to meet their self-absorbed make-believe worlds. I guess this is what happens when you raise a generation of mollycoddled kids who are use to getting a trophy just for paying a fee and participating rather than having to earn or work for it.

Recently, while reading, I came across something that was truly out of Alice in Wonderland. It seems there is a new "social justice" movement occuring on college and university campuses across the nation in which Black college students are demanding that they be segregated from white students, calling for "safe spaces" only for students of color. At Oberlin University, students have demanded "safe spaces" for black students only, as well as rooms in the library and science center to be used by black students only. They even want black/Africa only events at some universities and at Scripps and Pomona colleges, several such events have already occurred. The Afrikan Student Union at UCLA is asking for an "Afrikan Diaspora floor" as well as an "Afrohouse." The University of Connecticut is even building a new dorm for black students only. At California State Los Angeles, a new housing program opens up dorms for black students who want to be separated from the rest of the campus. A similar housing option is available at UC Davis.

HELLO, this is segregation. As a child of segregation and born in Memphis in 1962, this nothing to play with and not so simple a thing to be tossing around because somebody got their punk azz feelings hurt or micro-aggressed. It also seems as if these kids do not understand the historical precedents set in motion ex post facto Jim Crow regarding segregation and the concept of separate but equal. Let me remind your dumb azz. In the 1896 case of Plessy v Ferguson, the issue of whether public facilities may be segregated based on race was first proffered in the context of transportation. As a result of this case, the Democrat dominated Supreme Court said that the Equal Protection Clause was not violated by a Louisiana law requiring whites and blacks to ride in separate railroad cars. From this point on for decades to follow, the courts would hand down a series of decisions that permitted states to segregate people of color up until the 1930s when Charles Hamilton Houston of the NAACP started a surgical dismantling of the "separate but equal" position which defined Plessy. Segregation was rampant in public education from Boston and Maryland to Birmingham and Arkansas. The final nail in obviating segregation and the postulate of separate but equal occurred in 1954 when the Supreme Court decided the case of Brown v. Board of Education of Topeka. It was the conclusion and opinion of the Court that "Racially segregated schools" are "inherently unequal."

To be honest, I am bedeviled with what social justice means and what a social justice warrior is. First they can't be too social if they desire to be isolated from the world, nor concerned about justice if it is only interesting when black folks are killed by cops and not each other and warrior, I won't even go their (brave or experienced fighter). I mean they are afraid to live around people who have a different skin color than them and are even traumatized simply by reading the word TRUMP written in chalk. Likewise, I am trying to figure out what social justice work is for today it seems to be the exact opposite of what it was when I was raised as a child in the segregated south. All I can surmise is that it means tweeting a lot, making a couple-a-few hashtags, protesting and marching in the streets and crying and asking for space when you hear something you don't like. Clearly it doesn't involve patrolling streets in Chicago or Memphis, or volunteering to tutor at your local neighborhood school, or working in the jails, prisons and homeless shelters I prefer to spend my time in personally regularly.

The concept of self-segregation is weak and is in dialectical opposition to what Martin Luther King Jr. and other civil rights activist in the past envisioned regarding an America that was open to all without any barriers. Moreover it is comical for people to desire to be segregated while at the same time incessantly complaining and pointing out that they (blacks) are frequently excluded when compared to other students. I would wager if whites had a white only party these same kids would protest vehemently - maybe even saying that doing such would be a form of overt discrimination by other students and a sign of disrespect.

It is also evident that what some of these new age cats want is impossible and more unlikely than taking a yellow brick road to see a wizard. There is no constitutional right not to be offended. It is impossible to "bullet-proof" any person from reality.

No institution should be in the business nurturing idiotic preconceptions just because someone is uncomfortable. Moreover it is completely impossible to accommodate every possible example and or situation that might bother or upset someone: especially in places where folks are actively looking for things and ideas to become offended by. I just hope these soft as wet toilet paper social justice warriors that frighteningly and frenziedly represent the future coterie of African Americans, get a spine and learn to deal with knowing you cannot control everything and that are aware they are being pro-Jim Crow and black codes when they propose idiotic suggestions like self-segregation.

Yes, Our Generals Have Been Reduced to Rubbish

Rubble is a noun that describes waste or debris from the demolition of buildings in the form of stone, brick, and/or concrete. After saying U.S. "generals under Barack Obama and Hillary Clinton have not been successful," and that under their leadership "generals have been reduced to rubble, reduced to a point where it is embarrassing for our country" during a media extravaganza produced by NBC, Republican presidential nominee Donald Trump has been deluged with criticism for his assertions. Unfortunately criticism aside, there is both truth and merit to his statements whether the word used was rubble or rubbish.

By definition rubbish is something very bad, worthless or useless, it means that something has lost its utility (the state of being useful, profitable, or beneficial). If one looks at how the military leadership has been rendered impotent (utterly unable to do something for lacking in power and strength) he is correct. Since Obama began his term in 2009, with respect to the U.S. military and armed forces, one thing has been clear – he has removed more of the top military leadership brass than any president in modern times. Let us just look at his record to start with. Since taking office, high ranking military officers have been removed from their positions at a rate that has never been seen before by a U.S. President. It is somewhat reminiscent of what we have observed Erdogan do in Turkey. One report notes that President Obama has removed or purged the military of at least 197 top admirals and generals in his first five years.

Obama fired Rear Adm. Chuck Gaouette, commander of the John C. Stennis Carrier Strike Group, for disobeying orders when he sent his group on Sept. 11 to "assist and provide intelligence for" military forces ordered into action by Gen. Carter Ham. By the way, Gen. Ham was also relieved as head of U.S. Africa Command after only a year and a half because he disagreed with orders not to mount a rescue mission in response to the Sept. 11, 2012, attack in Benghazi.

Then there is the strange issue of President Obama's approach to defeating the Islamic State. It is well documented that President Obama typically silences any general that advises the use of US ground troops in Iraq. The Whitehouse has done this publically and behind closed doors. His consistent mantra, regardless of the advice of those with military and combat experience is that the US will not fight another ground war in Iraq nor will he put US boots on the ground.

This albeit US commanders inform him that it is improbably that the United States military will ever defeat ISIS via air power alone. Gen. Lloyd Austin was the top commander of U.S. forces in the Middle East and Gen. Martin Dempsey was the chairman of the Joint Chiefs of Staff from 2011 to 2015 both advised President Obama that ground troops would be required to defeat ISIS. Yet still, any advice offered that didn't match Obama's political aims (not military aims) were rejected, in particular the use of ground troops. Instead, President Obama unilaterally decided that he knew better and would only send an additional 475 U.S. troops to assist Iraqi and Kurdish forces. Even General Austin's predecessor, retired Marine Gen. James Mattis, said

Obama's decision not to send ground troops basically makes the mission to defeat ISIS improbable.

It is true Obama had to reduce the number of troops on the ground in Iraq, but namely because he failed to even try to argue against the levels outlined in the 2008 Status of Forces Agreement with Iraq. At the time there were around 45,000 U.S. troops stationed in Iraq and generals on the ground had requested a reduced number but did not foresee the military's troop-level going below 10,000. But such a number was too high for the Obama administration which preferred a number closer to 3,000, which meant that this was never a combat mission but rather served as a training only commitment.

The same can be said for the mission in Afghanistan. It is well know that the Afghan military do not have the necessary combat troop levels and power to protect every part of the country let alone to be in the position to effectively counter the Taliban. Gen. Martin Dempsey replacement, Marine Corps General Joseph Dunford during his confirmation hearing before the Senate Armed Services Committee, stated that he didn't agree with Obama's decision to pull all troops out by the end of 2016. His purview was that such a troop reduction seems to place policy over military implications.

This has been noted by several military experts. Retired Army Gen. John Keane, who devised the 2007 Iraq troop surge and has advised Afghan commanders in the past question Obama's approach to Afghanistan as well as Army Gen. John Campbell, the top NATO commander in Afghanistan, among others.

Keane pointed out that Gen. Campbell wanted to retain the current force of 9,800, but Mr. Obama "cut that in half," adding that President Obama frequently "does not listen to his combat field general," and on six occasions ignored "field commander recommendation on force levels for troops in combat." And like ISIS, the Taliban is becoming more brazen and powerful while claiming more area without any real push back from the Afghan security forces or police.

Obama's plan will have to depend on an unlikely assumption: that the formation of an inclusive Iraqi government under Prime Minister Haider al-Abadi can manifest. This is the only way President Obama will have any chance of defeating the Islamic State without U.S. troops being on the ground. This means that Prime Minister Haider al-Abadi will have to make significant inroads into healing sectarian wounds that were engendered by Nouri al-Maliki. But bringing the new Shia-led government to a Kumbaya moment with Iraq's Sunni minority may proffer to be a lot more difficult and could result in Sunni tribesmen moving towards ISIS instead of away from them. This approach is not only mousy and incoherent; it also involves serious risk (mainly having to depend on an incompetent and dysfunctional Iraqi military).

So Donald Trump may be more accurate than some may desire. When the President fires without hesitation, top brass the likes of the aforementioned, and never even considers firing or disciplining appointed member of his staff when they break the law, there has to be some additional motive and or reasoning behind such. The question is why deliberately reduce or military leadership to rubbish?

Gabon's Colonial Infection

Once upon a time ago, a cruel and barbarous colonial power came to Africa with its friends to rape and pillage and murder and spread disease. The year was 1839 and through the nefarious barrel of cannons, France forced the signature of a treaty with local chiefs that gave it power over the southern coastal regions of Africa which we presently call Gabon. The arrangement was made upon a gentlemen's agreement by Europeans at the Berlin Conference of 1885 which awarded all of the territory discovered by Pierre deBrazza to France. By 1910 this area would become French Equatorial Africa, and would encompass the separate colonies of Gabon, Congo and Chad. Fast forward to 2016, and although a semblance of independence has been achieved by Gabon and its fellow French colonized compatriots, nothing has really changed. Like the majority of African countries after colonialism, many in the west seldom hear of, mention or concern themselves with Gabon. In typical fashion, independence from France in this case only meant that the regular abuse and impoverishment of its population and rampant political corruption would happen under the rule of a fellow African instead of a European: an Africa which as in most examples is merely a stooge for the former pre-colonial power.

Gabon like much of ex-colonial Africa is a symbol of how a rich endowment in natural resources is used by the very few for their personal wealth while regular citizens struggle daily to survive. Although the nation has an illiteracy less than 3% and the population is generally well-educated, it has little economic growth namely due to French neocolonial economic policies and nepotism and inefficiency (despite as a nation it maintains the third largest hydrocarbon resources in sub-Saharan Africa). Just like most of the developed world, in Gabon the richest 20 percent hold 90 percent of the wealth with the rest of the Gabonese population fighting for scraps and living in poverty. This is why the protest have exploded to a new high after the recent presidential election in which many think Ping was defeated by Ali Bongo via classic sleight of hand corruption.

According to the constitution of 1961, Gabon is a republic in which the president and members of the legislature are directly elected. Leon M'ba, the first president of the republic, died in office in 1967 and was succeeded by Omar Bongo whom introduced a one-party system in 1968. Not until popular protests occurred in 1990 was Bongo forced to make revisions to the constitution to legalize multiple parties and reduce the term of office for president from seven to five years. Bongo, was the sole candidate in 1973, 1979, and 1986, yet was reelected president amid charges of fraud in multiparty elections held in 1993. His party won a clear majority in legislative elections held in December 1996 also but political unrest continued. In 1997 the constitution was revised again to re-extend the presidential term to seven years, renewable once, beginning with the 1998 elections, after Bongo won again.

Ali Bongo has been the President of Gabon since 2009 after his father, and then President Omar Bongo died. El Hadj Omar Bongo Ondimba had served as President of Gabon for 42 years from 1967 until his death. After weeks of violence, the Bongo family is cracking down on a popular protest in an effort to maintain its grip over the nation – a country his family ruled over the country for the last 50 years. However, this would be impossible to do if the family didn't have the tacit and overt support of France.

One could suggest that France is mostly to blame for this upheaval. Mostly as a function of an antiquated cold war-era policy known as "Françafrique," whereby France props up dictators in its former colonies in exchange for access to natural resources, military bases, and influence. In the case of Gabon, the country's uranium reserves have been particularly strategic for France. Gabon, like many other post-colonial African nations is a sad example of what has occurred throughout much of Africa, in particular Francophone Africa. Moreover, Gabon also has large oil reserves, but its people are poor, and the country has one of the world's highest infant mortality rates.

No matter what occurs, France will always be the main problem. Although it says politically it has attempted and desires to dismantle the incessant caricature of Françafrique, it has supported and continues to maintain a perceived invaluable yet operose relationship with the only family that has ruled the nation since its quasi-independence from France. The question is if Bongo is removed from office by whatever means, what would fill the vacuum? When France has tried to play the "I'm objective card" itself, it can't. Not to mention that France has to keep on propping up the governments of Mali and Chad as well because if they don't, like in every other place, radical Islamist movements would create terrorist safe havens and likely fill the void (something the Obama Administration has yet to learn).

But this is what history has shown us what France does. For example, after supporting a war in Biafra, overthrowing several presidents, collapsing Guinea's economy and bribing leaders to support its interests, France started to lose the control that it once exercised in Africa. This is probably why France uses extortion to make many African countries continue to pay colonial tax to France since their independence still today.

Anti-Bongo protests haven't let up and have been continuous and gaining momentum over the years, in particular from the younger generation of the Nation. Regardless of the opposition, all say Ali Bongo has not let go of the corrupt practices of his father, who amassed huge personal wealth and lived like a mob boss during his decades in power. Gabon has one of the highest per capita incomes in Africa, largely because of its oil reserves, but as mentioned previously, at least a third of the country lives in poverty.

So what's next for Gabon? Civil war is definitely a petrifying prospect. So is a crackdown that keeps the Bongo's in power. At some point, France will probably try to broker an outcome, but the situation may get out of hand. Omar Bongo ruled Gabon, now the continent's fourth-largest oil producer, for 41 years until his death in 2009. Add this to what all African leaders as well as the European political establishment are very much cognizant of (that nations like France need for their countries' resources); it is very likely that the sleight of hand European manipulation game of passing the buck, turning away the eyes and pretending to be objective will only continue.

I wouldn't be surprised if Bongo even adopted the same manipulation tactics once used on them by France. Take the example of Total, the third largest European Oil company based in France. Total is the oldest foreign petroleum company in Gabon and owns nearly sixty percent of Total Gabon, with the Gabonese government holding twenty-five percent and if estimates are correct, it produces between 200,00 to output to 500,000 barrels per day. This is a major card to play to maintain French support regardless of how oppressive the Bongo regime is toward its citizenry.

History has shown that when in trouble previously, France will do anything to make sure it has access to natural resources in Africa. When Africans under colonial rule were fighting to liberate themselves from European colonization, France would frequently use the French Foreign Legion to orchestrate military coups against presidents actually represented and selected by the people of those countries. In fact two such efforts were successfully implemented against the First Presidents of the Central African Republic and the Republic of Upper Volta (Burkina Faso). In total since independence from France, Coups have occurred more than 15 times in former French colonies.

But propping up Bongo and his lineage for the purpose of access to natural resources isn't anything new for France. The question is how will the everyday citizens of Gabon end this deadly infection?

Obama's Failed Putsch

A coup is a sudden and violent, seizure of power from a government. On occasion it has also been called a putsch. A little more than two months ago there was such a violent attempt to overthrow the government in the nation of Turkey. I heard about and read of several theories regarding the effort ranging from it being a theatrical production of Erdogan to a plan of secular aspects of the nation's body politic as formalized via the exiled leadership of the Turkish preacher, former imam Muhammed Fethullah Gülen. However, none of these are even able to approach being reasonable and logical in my estimation, notwithstanding they are somewhat plausible.

If you asked me, I would say it was planned by the Obama Administration in concert with NATO and implemented in the splendid tradition of the standard U.S. 'overthrow a democratically elected leader' playbook under the direction of the C.I.A. of course. And no, I have no explicit proof of this but history does support the tenable likelihood that I may be right and such is not farfetched at all.

Although I could give numerous examples, I would prefer to remind the reader of what we saw after World War II. After the defeat of Japan in 1945 when it was forced to leave Indochina. At the same time a movement was underway to free peasants in the region was taking off being led by Ho Chi Minh. Although US globalist history will claim that this was a communist led effort, the facts were that it was a grass roots operation.

As Howard Zinn noted, Minh, after he led the overthrew the Japanese, he established the Democratic Republic of Vietnam and issued a declaration of independence based on the U.S. Declaration of Independence and the French Declaration of Rights of Man and the Citizen. It was the first time ever Vietnam was free from foreign rule (and nearly foreign occupation) in history - however the West wasn't about to let this happen. At the time, the English was occupying South Vietnam, which they eventually returned to the French. Concurrently, Nationalist China under the leadership of Chiang Kai-shek controlled the northern part of Indochina, which the U.S. persuaded them to return it to the French.

To make a long story short, the U.S. did all it could to prevent Minh's desire of Vietnam unification and created South Vietnam as an American protectorate making Saigon head of the government under the rule of a former Vietnamese official living in New Jersey named Ngo Dinh Diem. Unfortunately Diem's rule was unpopular not to mention he was a Catholic in a country where most were Buddhists. And for that extra icing on the cake, he imprisoned all who criticized his administration.

In 1961 Kennedy became president and continued the policies of Truman and Eisenhower in the region. But by 1963 Diem had become even more autocratic and when a Buddhist monk set himself afire in Saigon to protest the artificially established U.S. government, it led to more monks committing suicide by fire to demonstrate their opposition to the government. With the approval and permission of the U.S. by Kennedy, American Ambassador Henry Cabot Lodge and a State Department official named Roger Hilsman, in concert with a group of Vietnamese generals began plotting a coup to overthrow Diem. The result was the assassination of Diem and his brother.

Now many may not see the similarities but for the purpose of brevity I will explain. The manner in which the opportunity arose in Vietnam for the U.S. to take advantage of a leader, whom in this case they selected and supported until his over-the-top autocratic rule and push for control was perceived as unacceptable by his citizenry, is ironically similar to the comportment of the citizens of Turkey with respect to Erdogan, albeit he was not handpicked by the U.S. he had been working on behalf (to what extent) of the military and geopolitical interest of the U.S., Europe and NATO.

Historically, when democratically elected governments (as with the case of Iran in 1953) or puppet autocratic states (as in Vietnam) and even states in between (as in present day Turkey and the Ukraine), the US will not hesitate to do whatever it can to protect the globalist oligarch and plutocrats of the political establishment and military industrial complex – even an invasion (as in the case of Iraq).

Historically for the U.S., the Coup has been and will continue to be the weapon of choice aside assisination to topple any nation that place their people before American and even western concern. Vietnam was just one example. We saw the same in Iran in 1953, where America (the CIA) spent millions to hire thugs and professional protestors to act out a real life overly violent protest across the streets of Tehran and this is based on the words of the CIA's Kermit Roosevelt. When loyal troops to the democratically elected leader of Iran Mohammad Mosaddegh got involved it became even more violent resulting in the deaths of hundreds eventually leading the forced resignation of Mosaddegh by members of parliament and others whom had been bribed by Roosevelt some weeks before. Why were these actions taken? So America and the U.K. could install their puppet Shah whom had agreed to restore Western ownership of the oil industry which Mosaddegh vowed to take from the west and nationalize it.

Then there is the example of Haiti in 2004 when hundreds of U.S. Special Forces worked with, trained and invaded the country from the Dominican Republic with anti-Lavalas. U.S. Special Forces were used to trained FRAPH militiamen and anti-Lavalas forces in the Dominican Republic. Upon which they invaded northern Haiti to set the groundwork for the overthrow of President Aristide. This approach is typical for carrying out a CIA ignited coup, in particular for Latin America, where they target nations that desire political and economic independence from the U.S. We saw this in Venezuela in 2002 and may be witnessing it currently. When successful, participants are rewarded with loot or positions of leadership (see Egypt's Abdel Fattah el-Sisi for one such example). In the end, the new leadership always ends up with the funding, backing and support of the U.S.

In the case of Turkey, I suspect that Erdogan bombing of U.S. supported Kurd's supposedly fighting ISIS in the North, and his increasingly dictatorial control on the country in concert with Americas need to have access to Incerlik air-field, everything came to boil.

Nonetheless, finding and instructing opposition forces and the promotion of violence and unrest in the streets is how the U.S. via the CIA create a state of emergency as a way to get rid of an elected or government and to gain power such that U.S. interest are paramount over the will and desires of said nation states. All that is left is the right time to take action to remove the government and install the coup puppet leaders in its place. We saw this work to perfection in the Ukraine where the Obama coup machine had its most successful outcome (too early to say regarding Yemen).

In January 2014 street protests turned violent in Ukraine. Most of it was by the hands of the neo-Nazi Svoboda Party and the Right Sector militia. Ironically the Right Sector militia had only been in existence for less than a year at the time and documents show that it is funded by Ukrainian exiles living in the west – mainly the U.S. and Europe (another typical CIA ploy). We know that the Obama administration via Assistant Secretary of State Nuland and Ambassador Geoffrey Pyatt that the Obama Administration were waiting for and anticipating a coup to happen in Ukraine.

These are just a few past and recent historic examples that are extremely well documented. This is why I am of the firm and assured belief that the Obama Administration was behind this. Then there is the photographic evidence that shows US Ambassador to Turkey, John Basse meeting with Turkish NATO Colonel Ali Yazici the day before the Coup attempt on the afternoon of August 7th. For the record Col. Yazıcı was one of the leaders of the coup and former military adviser to President Erdogan. According to reports, they met at Cengelkoy café the day before the coup.

I may not be able to prove it completely, but what we saw in Turkey had U.S. DNA all over it. It was a mirror image of what was observed in the Ukraine and to a lesser extent Iraq. And If may be honest, Syria as well, for we all know it is not improbable that the Obama Administration is supporting ISIS against Assad. I say this in all sincerity, for we knew Erdogan was sending weapons to ISIS and said nothing and Syria (Russia) just intercepted conversation between US forces and ISIS right before we bombed and killed scores of Syrian military fighters.

So say what you may, but I do believe the Obama Administration was behind this, what else can one expect from a president who is also a Nobel Peace Prize recipient?

How The Clintons Hooked-up With a Tyrant King of Morocco to Stack Loot

One thing about Bill and Hillary Clinton is that they are about getting that loot. Case in point among many glaring examples is their relationship with Mohammed the VI, King of Morocco. Now Morocco is no bastion of humanity, in fact it is one of the world's worst violators of human rights by some estimates. However, this did not stop HILLBILL from doing what they do, even while she was serving as the Secretary of State of the United Sates. It appears that while in office, Secretary Clinton often was in communication with lobbyist that served the interest of the King and country.

One of the prize possessions of the King is the state owned mining company OCP (formerly called the Office Chérifien des Phosphates). OCP operates in disputed international territory in an out-of-the-way part of the Saharan Desert that the Moroccan government seized after Spain withdrew in 1975. However, the government-owned mining company still extracts the resources in the region without adequately compensating the extremely poor people that live there and consequently, the King and the government have been condemned for these actions. In 2009 Forbes noted that the African nation controlled almost half of the world's phosphate deposits and that the year prior, had mined 28 million metric tons of phosphate rock, placing it only behind the China and the U.S. at the time. It must also be noted that King Mohammed VI, has an estimated net worth north of $5 billion.

Now while Hillary Clinton was Secretary of State between 2009 and 2013, the Government of Morocco was heavily courting the U.S. using the famous corporate law firm of Covington & Burling LLP, led by the firm's senior counsel Stuart Eizenstat. To be exact, Eizenstat represented OCP in Washington. Report suggests that the law firm was paid in upwards of $1.3 million since 2012 to lobby the State Department and other federal agencies by the mining magnet. After Clinton was in office, within a few months the Clinton Global Initiative restarted its foreign meetings as well as also resumed taking huge sums of money from new foreign donors. The Moroccan government is even on the record of providing monetary support for her presidential campaign.

As many have indicated, Hillary is very experienced in these matters. She must know that for years (when the CIA used Morocco as a Black site) that consistently the nation has been an incessant violator of human rights. In Morocco, thousands of children (mainly girls) are illegally placed in private homes of the elite as domestic workers, not to mention that there is no freedom of the press, speech or religion. Of the past few years, the state has increased restrictions on domestic and international human rights groups, for investigating how political dissidents, reporters and others are administered severely long prison terms without due process for what some have called "politically motivated offenses." In fact I am aware, at least some in the Clinton Stated Department knew for they categorized the government of Morocco in similar terms.

The same has been said about the company that made the $1 million donation to the Clinton Global Initiative Middle East and Africa meeting in Marrakech. The irony is that the Clinton's took the money when some few years earlier the Clinton's State Department had accused the Moroccan government of being corrupt. However, her criticism dampened and she praised not only the King and the Moroccan government, but also OCP. News and other independent reports note that OCP treats miner whom work in their mines inhumanely. They have been forced to retire early, had their pensions and wages cut dramatically and even state that many are often the target of forced detentions (especially Sahrawi's trying to obtain independence in Moroccan-occupied Western Sahara).

It is unlikely that Secretary Clinton or Stuart Eizenstat were ignorant of the nefarious activities of the government or OCP. Eizenstat is a close confidant of the Clinton's and served in multiple capacities under the Clinton Administration. This included serving as the United States Ambassador to the European Union, followed up with being Clinton's Under Secretary of the State for Economic, Business and Agricultural Affairs and ending up as Clinton's Deputy Secretary of the Treasury.

Without a doubt the country and OCP was aware of what such a donation would get – access and possibly changes in policy and the status in which Morocco was viewed by the U.S. State Department. Exports have pointed out that OCP has donated as much as $6 million to the Clinton Foundation over the past several years and openly, the Clinton's shower the king with praises including being a moderate ruler with whom the U.S. should partner with. However, this change in perspective is dubious given what was revealed in leaked Moroccan diplomatic cables that display that Hillary Clinton during her tenure as secretary of state on behalf of the nation lobbied UN to turn blind eye to their humanitarian abuses and violations in the Western Sahara. The documents also reveal that the Moroccan government had been occupied for years securing influence the Clinton family regarding dealings between the U.S. and Morocco relations, as well as to gain access to the ruling American elites in Washington, D.C.

One cannot over state this. First it is a fact that OCP CEO Mostafa Terrab registered with the Justice Department as a foreign agent for Morocco to help get the meetings started with representatives of the Obama administration. Second, the practice of foreign nations seeing and using donations to the Clinton Foundation to impact U.S. policy is so frequent an outcome, that it is not unreasonable for foreign interest to seek this method of operation of supporting the foundation as a means to achieve such goals. Lastly, entities of the Moroccan government hired a firm headed by Washington lobbyist Justin Gray ironically right after he was named a board member of the pro-Hillary Clinton Presidential super-PAC, Priorities USA.

I am certain many will suggest am just reaching and promoting a conspiracy theory when I am only outlining the way big money global politics happen in a world in which governments are run by crooks, thieves, plutocrats, corporatist and oligarchs. If I am incorrect, and there is nothing to see here and is not an indication of how the Clinton's, their foundation and globalist work, then explain to me how OCP, with all the controversy surrounding it, was able to receive nearly $100 million in U.S. taxpayer support, from the U.S. Export-Import Bank to purchase equipment from two American corporations? I am just asking.

America's Racist Baggage Today is the Legacy of the Democratic Party

It is very difficult for me to understand how inefficient the knowledge base of a sizeable corpus of individuals in the generations after mine have, as it pertains to history. No more astonishing a content area is this evident is with regards to American political history, in particular history of the Democratic Party. What few are aware of is that it is most probable that race relations in America are a direct result of Democratic Party policy and ideology. De Tocqueville acknowledge this when he stated that a natural prejudice was evinced against Africans brought to these shores against their will yet forever through pigmentation, will carry the "external mark" of a stranger, born in degradation considered as "an intermediate between beast and man." Taking this even further he wrote: "So those who hope that the European will one day mingle with the Negroes seem to me to be harboring a delusion...I see that slavery is in retreat, but the prejudice from which it arose is immovable...Race prejudice seems stronger in those states that have abolished slavery than in those where it still exist, and nowhere is it more intolerant than in those states where slavery was never known."

Ironically the laws that would manifest over his times and major attitudes regarding Africans in America, after the

Federalist Party, would be fostered by one party in particular as it pertained to policy – the Democratic Party.

That is correct; you name it, many of the collective political accomplishments that we as African Americans benefited from did not occur because of the Democratic Party but rather in spite of the Democratic Party. If it were not for U.S. Representative Justin Morrill (R-VT) in 1862, who got the Land Grant Act passed, which established colleges for African Americans, there would be no state funded historically Black Colleges and Universities. Even before this, the historical record notes that the Republican Party was formed essential to counteract the pro-slavery policies of the Democratic Party during a period in the nation's history in which we saw Democratic President Franklin Pierce signing the Kansas-Nebraska Act (which allowed for the expansion of slavery into newly acquired U.S. territories in 1854). Ironically the same year, Montgomery Blair, a republican argued in front of the Supreme Court on behalf of his client Dred Scott albeit it unsuccessfully where the record noted the only dissent with the court decision majority of seven democrats was Republican Justice John McLean.

Although many incorrectly believe that freed slaves were promised after emancipation and the 13th and 14th amendment 40 acres and a mule, this was never factually the case. The record documents that in 1866 Republican U.S. Representative Thaddeus Stevens introduced the legislation however it was vetoed by then Democratic President Andrew Johnson. Also that same year the Republican congress was able to override President Johnson's veto of the Civil Rights Act of 1866 and his veto of the Freedman's Bureau Act which was written to protect former slaves from Black codes put into law to deny rights granted by the 13th and 14th amendments. In addition, two times the following year, the Republican majority had to vote to over-ride Johnson's veto of the legislation granting African Americans the right to vote.

Being unable to compete with the Republicans in the Federal legislatures, the Democratic Party, in particular southern democrats whom were former confederate veterans found the Ku Klux Klan in Pulaski, Tennessee, on December 24, 1865. To be accurate, the Ku Klux Klan was founded and formed to be the military wing of the Democratic Party and actions around the nation after its inception until this very day still supports this objective. KKK violence was aimed specifically intimidate and kill newly freed slaves and Republicans. For example, in September of 1868 Democrats in Louisiana murdered around 300 African Americans whom attempted to defend their assault against a Republican Newspaper editor. The following month, while campaigning for re-election, Republican U.S. House Representative James Hinds was assassinated by self-proclaimed Democrats and KKK members.

Now I know many would say that this was decades ago and I would agree, but what must not be forgotten is that the plan desired (in concert with democrats) was to construct and put in place policy designed to disenfranchise and keep blacks from owing land and in a position to sustain ourselves. Moreover they wanted to defeat and keep Republicans equally at bay via terrorism. With the use of violence by the Party's military wing (the KKK) and separating blacks from their land and placing them in positions not being able to provide for themselves, they formulated new policy at the federal level designed to make blacks dependent on democrats and the government as opposed to truly exercising inalienable rights associated with actual liberty.

Republicans fought back with policy. In 1871 the Republican congress passed the Ku Klux Klan act which outlawed the Democratic Party military wing. Republican President even dispatched troops to South Carolina after democrats threatened blacks with death around the nation for even trying to vote. In one case, African American Republican activist Octavius Catto was murdered by democrats in Philadelphia. A few years later in 1874, nearly 30 were killed when democrats took control of the Louisiana state house because Republican Gov. William Kellogg dared to have an integrated administration.

When democrats returned to leadership, all of what had been put in place by Republicans was obviated. It was the democratic congress and President Grover Cleveland who repealed the Republicans Enforcement Act which gave African Americans the right to vote. Two years later America would see a Democratic Supreme Court uphold Plessy V. Ferguson. In 1901, Booker T. Washington would begin his life long battle protesting against the Alabama's Democratic Party refusal to allow African Americans to vote.

Even during the time of Franklin Roosevelt democratic policy was moving more towards the views of dependency politics advocated by the KKK in an effort to form a dependency class of Americans based on color alone. In 1937 it was the Republicans who organized against FDR's appointment of Ku Klux Klan member Senator Hugo Black to the Supreme Court and it was Democrat FDR, whom just three years later rejected the Republican Party's call to integrate the armed forces.

In 1953 California's Three-term Republican Governor Earl Warren wrote the land mark decision for Brown V. Board of Education after Assistant Attorney General of the Eisenhower administration Lee ranking argued the case on behalf of the Plaintiffs with Thurgood Marshall. On a roll it seemed, a Republican Federal judge, under threats from Democrats the blacks in the back of the bus law and ruled in favor of Rosa Parks.

History outlines democrats fought tooth and nail against all of these outcomes. After Eisenhower signed the

Republican's Party Civil Rights Act into law, he had to send the 82nd airborne division to Little Rock to enforce school desegregation amidst criticism from Democrats the likes of Future Presidents John Kennedy and Lyndon Johnson in 1957.

In simple terms, the legacy of racism that has it's weighted and oppressive foot on the collective necks of African Americans today was the courtesy of the Democratic party and democratic policy that continues to day with violence in the form of police brutality and disenfranchisement via policies of dependency. Andrew Hacker explained this in his 1992 tractate *Two Nations: Black and White, Separate, Hostile, and Unequal.* He noted that as African Americans, we must live in an existence that is far removed from free-will and free-choice. He wrote "Black Americans are Americans, yet they still subsist as aliens in the only land they know. Other groups may remain outside the mainstream but the do so voluntarily. In contrast blacks must endure a segregation that is far from freely chosen."

The reality is how America and Americans views race presently is a direct result of beliefs of a perverted democratic system that proffers race as its central element of contention. This contention is, when violence was no longer acceptable after the civil rights era, was transduced to policy designed with the intent to subjugate African Americans and systematically extract wealth from our community. As a policy this has never stopped. The most lucid view of this is the large urban cities of America. Cleveland has been run by democrats from 1942-present (police, city council and mayor) uninterrupted with the exception of 1972-77; Chicago has been run by democrats uninterrupted since 1931; Flint, MI since 1960; Detroit since 1962; Baltimore since 1967; DC since 1967; Philadelphia since 1952; Newark since 1953; and Milwaukee since 1960. And I would reckon if I had the time to look up a few things, I could find trend lines over the same period that would show an increase in poverty, unemployment, incarceration, high school dropout rates and poverty as well as decline in wealth, land ownership, housing and income too.

This is our biggest problem as a voting blocks today - Democrats running for state or national office aspiring to win black votes without appearing to give a FcK about nothing but our vote. So if we so upset about our current circumstances and conditions, why we still voting to enslave and impoverish ourselves by voting for democrats unconditionally? They gave us the politics of bigotry and oppression that is killing us currently.

Obama Didn't Found ISIS, He Just Breast Feed Them

A few weeks ago I read Republican Presidential nominee Donald Trump assert that President Barack Obama was the founder, or creator of ISIS. I just wanted to say for the record, I could not let this mistruth, as any mistruth stated by a politician regardless of party, pass without clarifying the record. What Mr. Trump forgets is that ISIS started long before Obama was President and in my view if we really want to know the deal, on its founding, birth or creation, we must go back to the Iraq war more than twelve years ago, under the Presidency of Bush 43.

As history has shown, the current leader of what we call ISIS is Ibrahim Awad Ibrahim al-Badry, a man we now refer to as Abu Bakr al-Baghdadi, the leader of the Islamic State. What is known about him before proclaiming himself the leader of DAESH is that in early 2004 he was housed in the infamous Abu Ghraib prison in Iraq. U.S. Defense Department reports note that coalition forces first captured Baghdadi on February 4, 2004, in Fallujah, Iraq. After the fiasco at Abu Ghraib, he was transferred to Camp. Bucca, located some 400 miles south of Baghdad in the southern town of Garma along the Kuwait border. It held some of the most radical extremists of the war.

One could argue that the procreation of what we now call the Islamic state begin when Camp Bucca was created and birthed during the peak of the Iraq troop surge in 2007 at a time when Bucca contained 24,000 – 28,000 inmates. It held both Sunnis and Shiites, who were separated because moderate Sunnis and extreme Sunnis and Shiites were at odds with one another. All and anyone who coalition forces figured look like the enemy or in the area of any type of bombing or sniper fire were rounded up in mass, in particular military-aged males, without due process since few if any U.S, military personnel spoke Arabic and all in general were incapable of distinguishing enemies for friendlies.

Detention facilities like Bucca played a major part in the rise of the Islamic State. After the Bush administration's policy of de-baathfication, what Bucca did was allow these individuals to link up with members of Saddam Hussein's ousted regime and develop new relationships. First it was unique, for as many have reported, it allowed for former Baathist secularists to get to know Islamist fundamentalists, both of which had nothing but hatred for the West and the U.S. Being once in politics and/or the military, the former Baathists provide jihadists with public relations, organizational and military skills. In the other side the jihadist were able to instill something to fight for in the former government ruling class of Iraq before the U.S. invasion and occupation. Some have estimated that nearly 90 percent of those freed from Bucca and other facilities returned to the battlefield to fight against coalition forces.

Like in America, prison served as a college or university for Islamic fundamentalism and jihadist training. In the long run, it would be these hardcore jihadists and former Iraqi military officials who would eventually become the leadership of the Islamic State. In Bucca, Sharia Law was instituted by radical extremist and fundamentalist which by some reports, even included gouging out eyes or cutting out their tongues for anti-Islamic behaviors considered to be Western in origin. A story reported by Al Jazeera based on first had reports suggested that jihadist were able to build relations and network in ways they would have never been able to do outside of Camp Bucca and that hard core extremist were able to radicalize other inmates and even give courses using the resources of the prison to teach inmates how to make explosives, and carry out suicide bombings. This is the start of what we currently refer to as the Islamic State and this was up to the year 2008, all of which was under the tutelage of George W. Bush.

Abu Bakr al-Baghdadi was not the only high profile prisoner detained at Bucca. Another was a former Iraqi military official who became head of the Islamic State's military council named Hajji Bakr and the future official spokesperson and a senior leader of the Islamic State Taha Subhi Falaha, commonly called Abu Muhammad al-Adnani al-Shami. Others included al-Baghdadi's deputy Abu Muslimal-Turkmani, Abu Abdulrahman al-Bilawi, the military leader responsible for planning the seizure of Mosul and the founder of the Syrian Al Qaeda affiliate al-Nusra Front, Abu Mohammad al-Julani.

Objectivity one cannot leave out the role that President Obama has played in nurturing the Islamic State. Since the CIA inspired uprising against Assad, Obama has been very busy sowing the seeds of war instead of diplomacy. It is clear that the reason for such are similar to the reasons he in concert with Hillary Clinton, led events that resulted in the murder of Libyan leader Muammar al-Gaddafi (with the use of Al Qaeda embedded in the U.S. backed opposition trained buys. special operation forces that had been inside Libya before the start of protests).

This is the plan they (Obama, Clinton, NATO and the West) have on deck for Assad and Syria as evidenced by leaked emails between Sidney Blumenthal and Obama's Secretary of State. Like Libya, Syria's Central Bank is state-owned & isn't controlled IMF (International Monetary Fund), has no IMF debt and more importantly maintains immense oil and gas reserves. Plus, being the only secular Muslim states in the Middle East, this gets in the way of the West divide and Conquer modus operandi. The first and last may be even more important than the two in the middle.

As of 2003, the only countries left in 2003 without a Central Bank owned by western interest were Sudan, Libya, Cuba, North Korea, Iran and Syria. After September 11th The U.S. was able to knock out two-for one by invading both Afghanistan and Iraq to then establish a Central Bank in those countries. Now back to Obama.

Obama is protecting Al-Nusura, Al Qaeda and ISIS-ISIL-Daesh by using the US Airforce to provide cover on behalf of terrorists invading a sovereign nation state for the reasons I stated above: it has nothing to do with protecting the citizens of Syria because if such was the case, the Obama Administration would bomb Saudi Arabia and protect the citizens of Yemen, whom the Saudi's are slaughtering with U.S. supplied planes, weapons, cluster bombs and White Phosphorus.

Although it was the Bush administration with the assistance of Dick Cheney, Donald Rumsfeld, and Paul Wolfowitz that broaden the idea of birthing terrorist organizations to fight U.S. wars under the name of freedom fighters, Obama took it to another level. Up until 2014, the Islamic State (ISIS) was called al Qaeda in Iraq (AQI). What President Obama breast fed with guns and intelligence, Al Nusra (an al Qaeda affiliate) is overnight called the "Moderate Opposition" and even worse, "The Free Syrian Army."

Either way it goes and regardless of what we call them, both are supported covertly by US intelligence and are merely malignancies of the same tumor – the Islamic State. Yes, Obama has got both his titties working: one for ISIS and the other for Al Nusra.

It is easy for the Obama Administration to keep on breast feeding these jihadist weapons especially since it is impossible to vet who is friend or foe (or rather foe or foe). Like any good hustler, anyone who is down to be a rebel no matter what we call them, get a gun and a regular salary know how to play the game and tell a random dumb American what they want to hear. And if they are not jihadist, the weakest of those the administration recruit cower under the first sight of ISIS extremist. Case and point was when U.S. officials reported openly that frequently, "moderate" rebels give up their weapons and vehicles to al-Qaeda. How else did ISIS get freshly FSA supplied US-made anti-tank TOW missiles ("Tube-launched, optically tracked, Wire-guided")? Also, they even openly admit to the media and U.S. representatives that they got no problems with al-Qaeda or ISIL and often work with and conduct military operations together.

The bottom line is that Mr. Trump is incorrect, it was the Bush Administration: specifically Dick Cheney, Donald Rumsfeld, and Paul Wolfowitz who founded ISIS. Obama did however, take the infant into his bosom and feed them when he took office. Now he and the rest of the West (many reluctantly) wants to place the blame what is happening in Syria at the feet of Russia when in actuality it is a consequence of Obama's foreign policy (or lack of) of aiding Syrian jihadists which has resulted in the intentional devastation of Syria, the massive migration crisis and the inordinate death toll of the nation's civilian population. Thus distinguishing between the FSA and al-Nusra is impossible, because they are virtually the same organization. Taking it a step further, it could be argued strongly that the moderate Free Syria Army is just a cover for al-Qaeda (al-Nusra).

The Russians are right: the Obama Administration has never had any desire or intention to defeat al-Nusra (as required by U.N. Security Council Resolution 2268 - 2016). President Obama got ISIS and al-Nusra sucking on his breast good and has them nearly strong enough to do his dirty work in his effort to destroy Iraq and Syria.

Paul Kagame and the Clinton's

For the Clinton's, especially President Bill Clinton, Rwanda has deep meaning for him and his presidency, for he has openly suggested that he will forever regret not intervening to prevent or maybe stop the Rwandan genocide, in which at least 800,000 people were murdered and/or killed in less than four months due to tribal genocide in 1994. At the time, then Vice President and Minister of Defense and now current President of Rwanda, Paul Kagame was a key player for both good and bad, depending on what side of the coin you end up on.

This has been the typical mantra of not only the U.S., but other western nations and leaders. For the Clinton's and the Clinton Foundation, he is considered to be among "the greatest leaders of our time, and described as a "brilliant man" who "freed the heart and the mind of the people." Historically the United States, Britain, Germany and the Netherlands, have always been behind Kagame's with former British Prime Minister Tony Blair describing Kagame as a "visionary". This is almost comical if it were not true that this is how many in the west really want and project for the world to see Rwandan President Paul Kagame in this manner.

Unfortunately the reality is that he is a dictator responsible for human rights abuses too numerous to list yet is a close associate of the Clinton's, the Clinton Foundation, and has received favorable treatment inclusive of funding by the Clinton State Department. Regardless of the fake picture they attempt to hide Kagame with, there is no way to get around that for him the democratic process in Rwanda is the equivalency of autocratic authoritarianism.

Since he has been involved in politics in Rwanda, dozens prominent dissidents have been tortured, disappeared, assassinated, and/or imprisoned. The lucky ones have fled the country or been exiled abroad. The list included journalists, opposition politicians and human rights activists. Thus it is for many, strange the extent of the relationship that Mr. Kagame and Mr. Clinton have. Kagame is a regular at the Clinton Global Initiative Annual meeting and even was awarded the organizations Global Citizen Award in 2009; Bill Clinton called him a "brilliant man" who "freed the heart and the mind of the people."

This unfathomable relationship and the depth of interaction and sway Kagame has with the Clinton Foundation regarding Rwanda has been maintained although the U.S. State Department has often been adjudged for wanting a third term as president in which he changed the constitutional amendment allowing him to do so.

To get a better understanding of how this relationship manifested, one can start in April 1994, when then Rwandan President Habyarimana's plane was shot down resulting in the deaths of Habyarimana and the President of Burundi, Cyprien Ntaryamira who was aboard the plane with him. Many believe that Kagame and the rebel army he led, the Rwandan Patriotic Front (RPF), were responsible. Since he has been in politics, the military wing of the RPF was renamed as the Rwandan Patriotic Army (RPA). After this incident, approximately 700,000–1,000,000 Rwandans were killed during the 100-day period from April to mid-July 1994. In fact since his entry in politics, dozens if not hundreds have been found dead under strange circumstances. Yet this has not stopped Mr. Clinton or the Clinton Foundation incessant encirclement of Mr. Kagame. Also, the United States remains one of Kagame's firmest ally and longest devotee (maybe because it is in its geopolitical interest seeing that Rwanda is a mineral-rich east African nation and maintains a powerful army).

Or it may be that the U.S. is alright with dictators it trains. Kagame studied at the U.S. Army Command and General Staff College in Fort Leavenworth, Kansas in the early 1990s, before he returned to Rwanda and seized power in 1994. His son even studied at West Point. On the other hand, it may be due to the large sums of money the U.S. gives to the Kagame government (although it is consistently cited for murder and human rights abuses). Much of this started under Bill Clinton and was supported by national security adviser Susan Rice and Jendayi Frazer, a former top State Department Africa diplomat. But it was not until Hillary Clinton became secretary of state that Bill Clinton was in a position to provide Kagame with even more loot by securing around $27 million from the State Department through a Boston-based charity that he ran. By the time secretary Clinton left office, she had allocated tens of millions of emergency funds to combat HIV infection overseas — called PEPFAR, for Rwanda although it maintained one of the lowest HIV prevalence rates on the continent.

But for as much as former President Clinton openly states he regrets his inaction regarding the genocide in Rwanda, the record clearly indicates he was more involved than either he recalls or wants to recall. First it was President Clinton who stopped the UN Security Council from organizing an intervention in Rwanda. To be more accurate, in concert with the British, the U.S., under the direction of then President Clinton were covertly funding and supporting the Kagame and his Army that invaded Rwanda from Uganda some several years prior. Secretly it was the desire of the Clinton Administration to keep Kagame as a proxy army to promote U.S. interest in neighboring countries. In addition Clinton had to be aware of U.N. evidence that senior Rwandan military staff who report directly to Kagame murdered tens of thousands of unarmed men, women and children, in 1996 and 1998. It was as if under the direction of President Clinton, Kagame became an official U.S. proxy along with Uganda and used to invade what is now called the Democratic Republic of the Congo (formerly Zaire) and first overthrowing Mobutu (1996), then Laurent Kabila (1998).

The end product allowed for the U.S. to have a major and dominant geopolitical imprint in the region, only at the cost millions more Rwandans, Ugandans and Congolese civilians dead and still to this day, incessant and ongoing conflict over the vast mineral wealth in that region of the Congo.

This is possibly why upon leaving the Clinton Administration in the capacity of Assistant Secretary of State for African Affairs, later, as U.S. ambassador to the United Nations Susan Rice allegedly tried to prevent the release of a 2010 U.N. report, about the murder and killings carried out under the instructions of Kagame. Of course Rice refutes this assertion although since the days of President Clinton and his wife's tenure as Secretary of State, the fact remains that unprecedented levels of funding continue to go to this despotic and murderous regime.

Having such a relationship with Kagame remains problematic for the Clinton's and the Clinton Foundation given the present leadership in the state department and U.N., as well as other nations in Europe and Africa note that the Kagame government continues to display a disregard for human rights, whether it is by providing weapons to rebels in the Democratic Republic of Congo or imprisoning and murdering his political rivals and/or suppressing political dissent and the press via violence. This will only get even more conflated if Kagame successfully amends the constitution of the nation to allow him to run for a third seven-year term (if he is successful, and Hillary wins the presidency, they will both be president starting 2017 together). This may not be a good look. We know in the past that the State Department under Clinton sidetracked a portion of US government grant money from nonprofit groups fighting HIV infection in Rwanda, and channeled it to the Rwandan government under the sole control of Kagame (US taxpayer money), which for the free thinking individual wreaks of possible favoritism and influence through his relationship with the Clinton's. Not to mention in 2012, Secretary Clinton boasted her work with Kagame in Rwanda as an example of the State Department assisting poorer nations to solve their own problems. However, she forgot to mention her husband's role in the entire effort. She lauded it as an example of the State Department prodding a poor country to take on more responsibility programs to fight HIV infection.

The bigger question is how long will these types of relationships (ones in which human rights are over-looked for personal gain and benefit) continue to go unexamined by the Clintons? Former president Clinton can pretend that he regrets not getting involved in stopping the genocide in Rwanda but the fact is he didn't give a fck. Clinton was not going to stop Kagame from finally overthrowing the existing, Hutu-led Rwandan government and seizing power. In reality, Kagame actions went better than expected based on U.S., and even some select European nations desires. So much so that a massive cover-up began at the International Criminal Tribunal of Rwanda, in which only Rwandan Hutus were indicted and prosecuted.

So any time former President Clinton says that he is sorry he did not intervene in Rwanda, it is frankly a bold-face lie. When he states he failed, what he really means is that my objectives were not to stop murder, but rather a means of implementing the good old fashioned U.S. proxy war to encourage repeated invasions of a sovereign nation (Zaire) – nothing more, nothing less.

Is Obama Just Stupid
Enough to want a war with Russia?

Growing up I loved movies, in particular gangster movies. One of my all-time favorites was *The Public Enemy* with James Cagney. The movie was about these two lifelong friends and their growth and maturation into the world of gangsterism during the time of prohibition. In many respects, it is all I can think about comparatively speaking when I think of the how Putin has been maneuvering himself in comportment when compared to President Obama.

Over the past few weeks, and some may say even two years since Russia began airstrikes in Syria, overtly supporting the sovereign nation state of under the leadership of President Bashar al Assad, the Obama Administration hasn't had any clear approach to Syria that can be honestly explained to the U.S. public – in particular since his "Redline" statement. Why is this?

Well to begin with, the Obama administration has no policy let alone any strategy to deal with what the U.S. has created in Syria. All that exist are goals, goals mainly proffered to accomplish objectives to benefit a select group of oligarchs more so than the citizens of Syria (who overwhelmingly support Assad) and the surrounding region or Americans. Attacking Assad was not only designed to accomplish regime change, it was also designed to do such in order to covet assets in the form of invaluable gas line routes, crude oil, gold and more importantly – to crush the state own National Bank of Syria.

I suspect that the powers that be via the current U.S. administration had a completely new landscape planned for the Middle East. Just taking a look at what has happened in Libya and Egypt for example makes this clear. However Vladimir Vladimirovich Putin has come to the stage.

Putin clearly isn't well liked on the world stage by the West, but he has positioned himself and Russia like Knights and Bishops on the chessboard of geopolitics like a Lasker defense and counter attack.

After Obama's classic 'redline' proposition, Putin made his opening mood by boldly going where no man has gone before – to openly stand with the sovereign nation of Syria and backing it up with his military apparatus. His next move was to have a closed door meeting with Obama to discuss securing the Syrian-Turkish border, although it may have been useless without the participation of Syria and Turkey. The objective for Putin was to try and end the continuous influx of arms entering Syria from Turkey and also expressing the need for "moderate" rebels to distance themselves from IS and associated Al-Qaeda derivatives. At the same time Turkey and Russia were on opposite ends regarding how they viewed the Syrian conflict, while Obama knew he needed Turkey to continue supplying weapons to ISIS.

Fast forwarding to the past few months and we have seen, Russia announce that they will be rebuilding its Soviet-era network of airfields in Vietnam and the northwestern Pacific island of Matua and that they conducted naval exercises in the eastern part of the Mediterranean Sea that started in August. This is in the background of Erdogan previously willingly expressing his views of President Obama and his policies in the Middle East. From Obama failing to withdraw U.S. troops from Afghanistan and Iraq to his support for Kurdish autonomy (without admitting such). Also, Erdogan has disagreed with the enduring economic sanctions from the West against Russia since the crisis in the Ukraine began.

Then the Coup attempt happened and mind you this was after the attack on Istanbul's Ataturk airport.

Erdogan made his first trip abroad since the July 15 coup attempt when he visited Russia, in which he had his first direct meeting with Putin since the shooting-down of a Russian fighter jet. Some are under the impression that he has Putin to thank for surviving the recent military coup and for even for saving his life (another reason his selection of Moscow for his first foreign visit since the coup is viewed with difficult eyes by London, Berlin, Paris and Washington-). Not only would this put a wrench in the region but it would or could upset the entire geopolitical landscape by rebuking the West and entering a closer relationship with Russia.

This benefits both Turkey and Russia and this fledgling Moscow-Ankara axis as Erdogan described it from an economic and geopolitical perspective. Moreover it allows Putin to highlight and disrupt U.S foreign policy inconsistencies and also those of the European Union.

We cannot forget that Turkey is a NATO member state and that the European Union needs the nation to serve as a shield between refugees and migrants from the Middle East to Europe. The posturing by the EU and their lucid desire to keep Turkey out of the club is being used by Putin equally as a postulate in his strategy. Now not only has Russia managed this, Putin has also been able to establish new relationships for Turkey with Iran and opened their perspective to a future Syria that doesn't require the ouster of Assad. In essence, Putin has altered the past 50-60 years of U.S. power dynamics in the Middle East in less than three months.

After Erdogan's visit to Russia, Turkish Foreign Minister Mevlut Cavusoglu met with his Iranian counterpart, Mohammad Javad Zarif in a meeting that resulted in both nations agreeing on more dialogue and cooperation on resolving the Syria crisis. It was the first meeting between top

Iranian and Turkish officials since the failed coup attempt. This was during the same week when Turkish Prime Minister Binali Yildirim said Turkey was willing to accept a role for Syrian President Bashar Assad during a transitional period. Ironically this came when Assad's forces started attacking Kurdish positions which may be an indication that a Syrian-Turkish rapprochement was underway (say goodbye to Kurdish autonomy in northern Syria).

The last nail was the Coup, which has provided the momentum for all of the aforementioned. Since this event, Turkey has incessantly carped about a lack of support from its Western allies and as with the rest of the world, has been watching EU's power shrinking in real time. Now true, some have suggested that Turkey is using Russia as some kind of leverage (Obama's state department word of the day) to place some heat in the Obama administration and EU after the coup attempt, but it seems in my opinion to be way more than that. It is also a reflection of Turkey's and Russia's perceived lack of U.S. leadership in the region with President Obama placing his tail between his legs when confronted with Russia on every major issue concerning Syria.

Since this, deeply anti-American sentiments and allegations that the Obama administration was behind the coup attempt (nearly 70 percent of Turks believe the U.S. was involved in the coup) and failure of the Administration to take serious (whether true or not) Erdogan's request for the U.S. to quickly extradite Fethullah Gulen has placed more distance between the U.S. and the Muslim Brotherhood-led government of Sunni Arab Turkey.

Just this past week, we saw Russia and Turkey signed an agreement to build a gas pipeline from Russia, called the Turk Stream pipeline which would bring Russian natural gas to Europe on a southern route that would bypass Ukraine with the main pipeline running across the bottom of the Black Sea.

Based on all of the aforementioned factual observation, it is no wonder why President Obama would do anything, even something stupid, half-baked and witless as to even speak of taking military action against Russia, sadly as well, over any provocation (bombing parts of West Aleppo occupied by ISIS and Al-Nusra to a make believe propagandized hack on the Clinton campaign).

I should have seen this coming. Ever since Obama touted his so-called Russian 'reset' all we have seen from the Administration is Russia raise their flag over Crimea and more bungled relations with the Russians (clearly a major failure of Obama's foreign policy). Seems as if President Obama is no longer in charge of any of the activity regarding Russia or anything involving Syria. This is true for his activities at home, with the coalition and even NATO. What we are presently viewing in Syria may be one of the most unstable and hazardous geopolitical situations in modern times, at least since the last World War. On the surface, it is more than evident that Obama or his handlers are pushing the limit with Russia. From the war games NATO is conducting in Russia's backyard to the massive influx of U.S. and NATO troops into the Baltic States and elsewhere in Eastern Europe. And in Syria, suffice it to say the administration never wanted a ceasefire in Syria anywhere.

Before this week there was a bellicose Ambassador Samantha Power (who ran over a child and killed him with her car in Africa recently) calling the bombings in Russia barbarous and the suspension of military contact between the U.S. and Russia. Now we hear U.S. intelligence officials (without evidence) accusing the Russian government for being responsible for recent hacking in an effort to disrupt America's political process. One has to ask why is there such an angry and aggressive tone coming from the Whitehouse?

For one, President Obama has spent a lot of loot arming the rebel in Syria, in particular Jabhat al-Nusra and the Obama administration will continue to support Jabhat al-Nusra and even call the "moderate rebels" or member of the "Free Syrian Army" when a name change will never obviate the reality that they are still al-Qaeda and/or a part of al-Qaeda in Syria. Abual-Ezz, a major commander of the group has gone on the record and has openly stated that his organization is part of al-Qaeda. Thus the folk that the Obama administration is supporting with weapons are an affiliate to the terrorist organization the United States has been at war with since 9/11 – as a recently leaked Hillary Clinton email reveals. On the opposite end Russia is fighting the groups that the United States are funding and arming. So in essence we have is a rebel group funded and backed by the United States fighting against the Russians and Syrians.

The Obama Administration needs to stop arming and funding the Jabhat al-Nusra and discontinue this idiocy directed towards Russia because if this doesn't stop, Obama's will be leading the nation closer to World War III. What we need to do is to fight on the same side as Russia and Syria, considering that they are actually targeting al Qaeda and ISIS, but this makes too much sense. The problem is that even when President Obama leaves office, if Hillary wins, she will carry on what Obama has started.

What is clear is that Putin has taken the lead in this race and that it may be a premonition of things to come regarding U.S. and Russian interaction on the world stage. Obama, neoliberal, neocons and Clintonites are occupied with the goal of U.S. military intervention and aggression against Syria although it may lead to a war with Iran and Russia. I don't understand why, although I outlined a few reason and known facts in the beginning of this essay. Not to mention, Putin has been basically pimp slapping Obama around the room like he was James Cagney smashing a grapefruit in Mae Clarke's face.

I Don't Get Down Like That

Now how can I say this? Mr. President, respectfully, I ain't your bich and I could give a hoot about your legacy. And if I may keep it 100, in all honesty your legacy don't amount to feces for any black person in America, with the exception of cats fortunate enough to have landed on the payroll of your administration and staff.

What is your legacy from my objective purview you might ask? Well first, since you took office, the seasonally adjusted labor-force-participation rate for black Americans across the board has declined and the number of black food-stamp participants has increased more than fifty percent. Add to this that the percentage of black Americans who own homes has declined sharply and that real median income among black households based on data from your Census Bureau has also declined, I'd say your legacy for a Nobel peace prize winning president for black folk is rather FCKD. One reason I find it hard to believe you could even form your lips to utter the statement: "Like the rest of America, black America, in the aggregate, is better off now than it was when I came into office."

In general, even if you are not black, Bureau of Labor data notes that folks you claim to care about the most and structure your economic policy around to assist in the lowest income brackets, have suffered the most under your presidency. But this all makes since by my understanding of basic math for poor job growth and a sharp reduction in labor participation rates can only have one result – the reduction in real household income.

Now it appears as if you have a few additional problems with your legacy. Between you and the Federal Reserve bank trying to paint a rosy picture of the U.S. Economy (although it is not a sign that the labor market is improving when it is being filled-up by part-time jobs and cats holding more than one of said part-time jobs), your administration just ran an additional $587 billion budget deficit for the past fiscal year (about a thirty-four percent increase). Mr. President we both know that artificially low interest rates, if they continue will only result in one outcome – hyperinflation. Frankly, the majority of this political dysfunction is at your feet and remains a real threat to the viability of the U.S. economy.

If you would take the time to just compare the two year Treasury yield against the ten year Treasury yield you would be able to see this. I am certain you know such economic indicators impact blacks at a more devastating level than the general U.S. populous; like they say we the last to be hired and the first to be fired. For example, currently we have the most multiple job holders since the recession of 2008 started and this number is steadily growing. This means a higher poverty rates for blacks since 2008, a reduction in the number of young black men with full-time employment and an increase in median white wealth providing them with more income at a pace way surpassing that of blacks under your administration. This is without me even mentioning the paltry rate of GDP growth since you took office.

Most Americans and even more blacks have entered in some form of debt collection. If the overall proportion of U.S. citizens in debt collections is thirty-five percent, just imagine what the proportion is for black Americans.

Don't take my word for it, a recent study entitled *Problems Unsolved and a Nation Divided* published by your Alma mater, Harvard University confirms my observations. The research indicates that your economic policies are basically serving to leave many Americans behind in the prosperity your policies have provided for the top one percent. The authors also note that the U.S. economy under your leadership has as continued to wane in the aftermath of the financial crisis of 2007-08. From their perspective, most of this is a consequence of failed leadership in the economic realm and a lack of an economic strategy from the federal government because the administration's sole policy is to leave all economic policy decisions to the Federal Reserve via monetary policy alone. This means that our main problem is that job creation (the fact that job creation has failed to recover to the levels experienced prior to the financial crisis of 2007-08).

So again, Mr. President, I'm not your bich and you don't have the authority to order or beg me to vote for you bottom bich. I am neither your slave nor your trick – I don't get down like that.

From Brown shirts to Never Trump

I am an admitted history addict. I in particular have a keen passion for the Vietnam War, the Zulu Wars and World War II. It is not the wars singularly that attract my attention, but rather events of political and strategic inferences that may have an impact just as significant as bombs and guns. With the Vietnam War it was how the U.S. placed a puppet from New Jersey to run Saigon, Vietnam in the capacity of president and the use of Napalm and Agent Orange on innocent civilians. Regarding the Zulu wars, it was the two-facedness (if such is a word) of Theophilus Shepstone and Henry Bartle Frere. With respect to World War II, it was the 761st Tank Battalion and the rise of the Sturmabteilung (SA), the precursors to the Schutzstaffel (SS) – what we commonly now call the "Brown shirts" (Braunhemden).

It is difficult for me to watch what is going on today (with the animosity and vitriolic level to which emotions have come about as a consequence of the 2016 presidential campaign) without being reminded of the SA and SS during the end and after the fall of the Weimar Republic. Both the SS and SA were major contributors to Adolf Hitler's rise to power during the 1920s and 1930s. They had several functions of which the most significant being attending rallies of opposing political parties and campaigns as well as provide protection for Hitler and the upper leadership of the National Socialist (Social Democratic Party of Germany). Through violence, the Brown shirts attacked and intimidated members of rival political party's including but not limited to the Communist Party of Germany as well as Black, Slavic and Romani citizens, unionist and of course Jews and gypsies.

Although I have frequently heard rhetoric describing Donald Trump as a fascist or that his supporters are violent in the tradition of the Nazis (Social Democratic Party of Germany), I must honestly say that the term is more appropriate when describing the violent actions of Anti-Trump and "Never Trump" protestors. Now true, some Trump supporter inside of his events, have acted like cowards and attacked idiots that go inside to protest, but I have yet to see any Trump supporters lay in wait and attack individuals who just want to see Secretary Clinton Speak.

From New Mexico to California I have seen behavior that was not becoming of civility and respect and it was not coming from Trump supporters. In Albuquerque during a Trump rally at the Convention Center, what started as a peaceful demonstration outside of what has been reported of around a thousand protestors, ended with said protestors throwing rocks and bottles in the direction of police and burning Trump paraphernalia. At a rally held in Anaheim, multiple arrests were made for similar behavior.

In Costa Mesa, anti-trump protesters stomped on cars, threw rocks at motorist passing by, stopped traffic and destroyed city property by slashing the tires of police vehicles and smashing windows resulting in damage to at least five police vehicles according to reports. In San Jose demonstrators attacked Trump supporters with eggs and water balloons, snatched signs and hats off supporters' heads and this was the non-violent portion of the mobs. Eventually Trump supporters were surrounded, jumped and/or sucker punched as they left the rally.

One was captured on camera showing a Trump supporter hit solid over the head as he was walking away from a group of protesters which left him bloodied. Another was attacked, had his shirt ripped off of him and beaten bloody by anti-Trump protestors. We have also seen progressive anti-Trump activists attack his motorcade and supporters in Minneapolis recently in which we also saw more public attacks on a Trump supporters , and an apparent theft in public from a Trump supporter being escorted into the event. Reports also point out that some fundraiser attendees were spit on and verbally assaulted as they left the convention center. One could only imagine if this had happened to the Hillary Clinton motorcade or her wealthy Upper East Side campaign contributors. To top it all off, just this week there was a fire-bombing in North Carolina on a local Trump/Pence and Republican Party headquarters in in Hillsborough, North Carolina. A wall to an adjacent building was spray-painted with a swastika and the words "Nazi Republicans leave town or else."

This is really bazar, in particular in America. And I know there are many who will say it is because of Trump's talk and his words, that he is responsible for the violence. But to abrogate individual personal responsibility for violent behavior is never appropriate. It was assertions like these by the network media outlets and white citizenry that were stated when similar events happened to the NAACP. It was because of their words about freedom and liberty mentioned by Harry T. Moore that resulted in him and his wife dying after they were the victims of a bombing of their home in Florida on Christmas night 1951. Ironically by member of the military wing of the Democratic Party – the Ku Klux Klan. These were the first NAACP members to be murdered for their words and actions.

Then there was Vernon Dahmer, president of the Forrest County chapter of the NAACP in Hattiesburg, Mississippi who on January 10, 1966 had his home firebombed by the KKK and died as a result of his injuries for speaking out – just speaking out his own views and beliefs. Just one year later Wharlest Jackson, Sr., a NAACP official in Mississippi died when a car bomb exploded while he was driving. I am not comparing the events of what recently happened to these actions of the past but I am attempting to demonstrate what intolerance looks like in action no matter who commits such actions. This is my view and it is consistent regardless of race. But it seems there is an intentional and overt attempt to get folk riled up in such a manner that will produce hate.

Recent evidence suggests that the DNC in concert with the Clinton campaign have even planned anti-Donald Trump protests. Based on the release of Democratic National Committee emails by WikiLeaks, multiple DNC emails show party top leadership approving and knowing of two planned anti-Donald Trump protests in Indiana and Montana to the point of sending interns. There is also evidence that people have been paid to protest at Trump events and that advertisements have even been taken out on Craigslist. One gentleman Paul Horner stated that he answered a Craigslist ad about a group needing actors for a political event and was paid $3,500 to protest a Donald Trump's rally in Fountain Hills. Discussing his training he stated, "I learned they only paid Latinos $500, Muslims $600 and African Americans

$750." Another Craigslist supposedly offered people $15 an hour to protest at a Trump's rally in Janesville, Wisconsin.

All of the aforementioned is sickening to the stomach and I cannot see in any way, form or manner that such behavior is acceptable. It isn't about Trump or Clinton from my perspective, but rather about civility and the respect that comes from the human decency of treating others as you would like to be treated. I may not support that you support or even vote for who you are voting for but I will not attack you, call you names or go on or damage your property because I disagree with you – this is simply childish. Never ever will there be any justification for such actions and behavior. In particular actions that result in physical harm to people. It is in no way respectable to ask for other to accept you, in particular if you are a minority in America yet you have no desire to accept difference in others, even difference in views, beliefs and opinion.

It is duty to all civil minded people to always reject violence, in particular political violence. One should not have to risk assault for openly supporting their political candidate of choice, or have their yard signs stolen or even burned. The reality is albeit we throw the word fascist around all willy nilly, 99.9% of the folk that use couldn't define what it means and as George Orwell wrote in 1944, it is a term that has been used to socialist, conservatives, Catholics, nationalist, anarchist, communist, laborist and unionist. But one thing for sure, the majority of the folk who express freely and openly their support for one candidate or the other are not fascist, not even the majority of Trump supporters. As simple a statement as it may be, Rebecca Black was right when she stated, "The fascist of the future will be the anti-fascist."

Why do impoverished Black people support Hillary?

When I think of Hillary Clinton, and the strong support she has from black people, it simply blows my mind. Here is this woman, an elite northern school graduate from middle class Chicago whom was not only president of the young republicans but also a Goldwater girl in 1964 in the form of both volunteer and supporter. In case you may have forgotten, Barry Goldwater was the first Republican to win the deep South since Reconstruction by campaigning to defeat the Civil Rights Act and consequently was the main person whom motivated Hillary Clinton to get into politics.

As expected, black politicians have lined up in like they were camping out to get the latest IPhone or new pair of Yeezies to endorse her. It is as if by doing such and showing your loyalty to master, she will let you move into the big house as a reward for being faithful to the Clintons. This was the way it was in 1992.

In 1992 when black folk put Bill Clinton in office in addition to some theatrics of his own (playing the saxophone on the Arsenio Hall show and walking up to an American citizen during the debate to answer questions directly), African American communities across America in rural and urban areas were suffering and had been devastated economically. If one is old enough to recall, one reason for this was Bill Clinton's ability to say things to the black community that he would say in opposite to white communities. On the same day in the morning Bill Clinton would be singing Lift Every Voice and Sing at a NAACP or black Baptist church meeting and later on that night speaking to a room full of Dixiecrats tell them how he was willing to be tougher on crime and make our cities safer than republicans ever could.

Bill, the democrats, the service economy, big banks, Wall Street and the average white American won but not black folk, we got the shaft. The late 1980s and early 1990s was a period of mass losses in factories across the nation and the diminution of U.S. manufacturing. All because big corporations were moving abroad as a consequence of globalization and in search of cheaper labor and fewer regulations. This continued at an even larger scale and greater pace with Clinton as President.

At the start of his presidency, America saw unemployment rates among young black men multiply to pornographic levels. As a direct result, crime increased and we were watching the start of the crack cocaine epidemic. Now Blacks were in essence caged in segregated public housing hoping that the Democratic president would do something to help as he promised during his campaign. He was able to secure 83 percent support from black voters in 1992.

Unfortunately under the Clinton regime we observed the largest increase in federal and state prison inmates in American history. He was firmly in support of the sentencing disparity for crack versus powder cocaine, which not only resulted in disproportionate arrest and sentencing for African Americans, it also increased funding for drug-law enforcement as a continuation of prior republican administrations war on drugs. He also pushed for a federal "three strikes "law and in 1994 he signed a $30 billion crime bill that mandated life sentences for some three-time offenders, and provided $16 billion for state prison grants and the expansion of police forces among other things.

By 1996, after securing eighty-four percent black vote to gain a second term and using coded language about race (crime, welfare, crack cocaine) to divide the nation and divert attention from the economy that worked only for the top one percent, the federal the penal budget became twice the amount that had been allocated to food stamps.

The next move for his administration was to cut billions from public-housing and child-welfare (Aid to Families with Dependent Children - AFDC) budgets and have them re-directed to increasing incarceration. In fact, Clinton cut funding for public housing more than sixty percent ($17 billion) while increasing funding for prisons by more than 170 percent ($19 billion).

So what Bill Clinton supported from a policy perspective was what democrats in large urban areas had been supporting for the prior 50 years - discriminatory laws that keep black and poor people in their place while extracting lifeline resources that serve to sustain people during times of economic hardship. But this wasn't enough for him; he had to go even beyond cruelty.

Next the Clinton Administration eliminated Pell Grants for prisoners seeking higher education to prepare for their release and overtly supported laws that would make it easier for public-housing agencies to deny shelter to anyone with any sort of criminal history.

It was President Clinton who proposed the "one strike and you're out" initiative, which meant that families could be evicted from public housing because one member (or a guest) had committed even a minor offense – this was his brainchild. No black men whom had been released from prison with nothing could any longer return home to family if they lived in federally assisted housing or else the entire family would be kicked out. On top of this, the Clinton Administration promised, signed into law and made certain that anyone convicted of a felony drug offense would never be able to get federal financial aid if you had drug convictions. He signed into law a lifetime ban on welfare and food stamps for anyone convicted of a felony drug offense.

When Bill was finished, more than half of working-age African-American with criminal records was now by legal sanction, burdened with congressional and presidential approved discrimination in housing, employment and access to education. Moreover, after his two terms as President, Clinton left the nation with the highest rate of incarceration in the world, thanks to his 1994 Crime Bill which saw conservatively, more than 80% percent of all drug offenders sent to prison being black men and the unemployment rate for non-college-educated black men (including those behind bars) being north of 40 percent - all with the approval and support of the current democratic nominee Hillary Clinton and the unusual accomplice of the black vote. Now I know many will say that this was Bill and Not Hillary. Truthfully they are one in the same – HILLBILL.

So all I am asking is what have the Clintons done to keep black folk voting for them other than belong to the Democratic party? Why do impoverished Black people living from paycheck to paycheck support Hillary Clinton?

The housing bubble that precipitated the crash that created the great recession was done mostly on the backs of people of color. The bankers who profited from preying on the black communities got bailed out to the tune of trillions of taxpayer dollars; their victims mostly lost their homes. The perpetrators were never even indicted by the Obama administration, which had been tight with Wall Street from jump.

And it is bazaar how folk forget how she and her husband went after then Senator Obama. In 2008 while campaigning in South Carolina Hillary suggested that Dr. King's dream was wasn't anything without President Lyndon B. Johnson passing the Civil Rights Act. Tim Russert, then the host for NBC Meet the Press said it was as if she was saying "it took a white man to get blacks to the mountaintop." Then there is what Bill Clinton was reported to have said after it was reported in 2010 he was upset that Senator Ted Kennedy endorsed Barack Obama over Hillary. In the book *Game Change* written by John Heilemann and Mark Halperin it is reported in a conversation with Kennedy he said, "A few years ago, this guy would have been getting us coffee," describing Senator Obama. We won't even speak on her dismal record with Black New Yorkers or Blacks across the nation while she served as the Senator from New York.

The simple truth is that Black Americans have been voting for the Democrats consistently for more than the past forty years and we have little if anything to show for it with the exception of a few Attorney Generals, a President, and a museum. Why, because economically, we have been shown but fail to acknowledge that the economic positions of the democratic clearly elucidate it as being the party of the affluent white collar white and no one else.

How can we forget or ignore that it was the Clinton administration that deregulated banks and Wall Street which was a major factor in the financial crisis the U.S. experienced in 2008 and had a more than disparate impact on African Americans compared to any other ethnic racial group in the country. And his relationship with Wall Street and Big banks is no different from his wife. How else can folk get upwards of $250,000 for forty-five minute speeches without doing any actual work? The role of the practices of big banks and Wall Street on the African American community cannot be denied yet she panders to us like the man on the corner begging for some change. She may speak out about redlining practices that are discriminatory and illegal and predatory lending but the only time we see or hear from her, like most other democrats is when they want our votes and support while at the same time she is all buddy-buddy with the folk who are making it extremely hard for African Americans (the people she called super predators and deadbeats) to obtain a fair and equal economic footing in America. So again I just ask why impoverished Black people support Hillary Clinton?

For more than 40 years her party has collectively siphoned the African American vote without returning anything in exchange for our continuous and even subsistent electoral support and what have we received or to show for it economically? A few social programs designed to make us helpless and dependent on government, the status of a permanent status as secondary class citizens in America just like during the Black Codes and Jim Crow, and historically high levels of crime in our communities, unemployment, poverty, incarceration rates, poorer health and wellness status and mass illiteracy.

I take it these basic public benefits are the aspects of Hillary Clinton's policy that excites you and her base – have at it. Personally I deserve better and much, much more.

Obama Leading From Behind in the Philippines

Last week President Rodrigo Duterte of the Philippines and Chinese President Xi Jinping held talks in Beijing. Although only in office for less than four months, Duterte's words and actions have managed to disrupt the traditional Washington and Manila subtleties and have actually added some spice to President Obama's last few months in office not to mention his Asia strategy or pivot which was supposed to mark a shift in American foreign policy from the EU and Middle East to the Asian Pacific rim nations.

President Obama began this effort somewhere around the time he had become embroiled in Syria and had failed to keep his word regarding a "Red Line" in the region. More specifically we can point to the report from the June 2013, the Asia-Pacific Strategy Working Group at the American Enterprise Institute called Securing U.S. Interests and Values in the Asia-Pacific that was submitted jointly to congress and the Whitehouse (in my view, the brainchild of Robert Kagan (Director of the Foreign Policy Initiative) and Assistant Secretary of State for East Asian and Pacific Affairs Kurt Campbell).

In geopolitical terms all bull shi* aside, the pivot has mainly been implemented because the neocons in the Obama Administration and elsewhere inside the beltway know that all of the Pacific Rim and Southeast Asian nations wants a better relationship with China, and the U.S. must do all that it can to keep China second fiddle to American interest. Moreover, it is imperative that the U.S. attempts to keep a major presence (policy wise and militarily) in hand with respect to our relationship with China -- which continues to become more complex economically in terms of national security. With the recent changes in policy regarding Duterte, this all seems to show that the Obama Administration wasn't playing with a full house or flush but was rather bluffing and it only took Duterte's recent statements to bring all of this to the surface.

So far there has been no official word from Obama's Whitehouse or Department of State on where we stand with respect to this so-called Asian pivot. Some may consider the newly elected president's actions strange given the footing his nation and the Chinese have had over the past decade – in particular actions related to access for Filipino fishermen to Scarborough Shoal, which China seized in 2012. According to reports the meetings focused on economic aid to the Philippines and coming up with a more productive manner in which to address and deal with the South China Sea issue with respect to territorial disputes and avoiding confrontations with the ten-member Association of Southeast Asian Nations.

These actions make it very difficult for Obama and the U.S., if America wants to maintain U.S. forces at Philippine military bases. But if Duterte's statements are accurate when he asserts that he would prefer to end all and any future military cooperation with the U.S., the so-called Asian pivot is now more like a moon walk. Duterte also publically stated his desire to have all U.S. counterterrorism troops out of his country not to mention his disdain for Obama having the gall to be critical on his war on drugs and crackdown on drug dealers and users. One could say President Obama brought all of this on his self when Duterte approached him during a dinner at a regional summit in Laos and Obama sent him to meet with another subordinate member of his White House staff.

I don't claim to know much about Duterte but I am somewhat knowledgeable of Filipino history; as too is Duterte like many children that recall the history of collective oppression under the thumb of imperialistic and colonial foreign rule the likes of Theodore Roosevelt and William McKinley. The U.S. had always desired to take territories in the area of the South pacific and our occupation of the Philippine Islands occurred after the Spanish-American war of 1898-99 when we took the island nation from Spain after Admiral George Dewey sailed into Manila harbor in 1898 with a fleet of American vessels and destroyed the Spanish ships anchored there.

Obama's failure in dealing with President Duterte can simply be reduced to Obama's lack of knowledge about how deep the historical anti-American sentiment is for 99 percent of the Filipino people; how they will never forget the first American soldiers landing in the Philippines in 1898 and how President William McKinley wanted to seize the entirety of the archipelago for the United States saying it was his Christian duty. They never have forgotten how the American soldiers called them "niggers" or how between 1899 and 1913 the United States of America for conquest sake, killed more than 400,000 Filipino fighters and more than a million Filipino civilians via America's scorched earth policy, intentional economic hardship, mass killings and vile murderous butchery (something still to this day, the U.S. Government has not apologized for).

Obama also has not paid attention to how popular the new President is and the extent to which is policies have been well received by his electorate. In about four months, Duterte's has already put in place new policies to tackle tax reform which includes cutting personal income taxes to 25% from thirty-two percent in an effort to help the middle class. The overall objective of his ten-point economic agenda is to lift 10 million Filipinos from poverty by 2022. He has also put in place policy to help indigenous people displaced by mining and logging so that they can return to their ancestral lands and has started a program of free medical checkups for the 20 million poorest Filipinos. Add to this his open commitment to provide free irrigation to subsistence farmers, it is no wonder he is so popular. Even with the condemnation from the international and western community, national data show his popularity for his policy (even his drug policy) and presidency is extremely high. Then there is the relationship I spoke of to begin with. Not only is he taking a hand away from the U.S. and extending it towards China, he is now saying he desires closer and more permanent ties with Russia. This would be worse that Duterte calling Obama "son of a whore," it would down right like a pimp slap.

Before the statement could be printed in the western press, Putin via the Russia's ambassador to the country promptly said Moscow was down and ready to fully cooperate with Manila stating "Formulate your wish list. What kind of assistance do you expect from Russia and we will be ready to sit down with you and discuss what can and should be done."

Some may say that this is another example of Obama leading from behind. With all that is going on from Yemen to Syria to the South Sudan and now the Philippines, it seems that the presidents' Asian policy is floundering and reflective of his approach to foreign policy in general – doing something but not having a follow up plan to carry out said policy.

We have seen this in Libya, in Syria, the Ukraine, South Sudan, Russia and now again with the Philippines. The question is what will U.S. relations with Manila be like in the future for our next president? Clearly Obama doesn't care seeing that all he does and has been doing is campaigning. To date, with the exception of a few nations, Obama foreign policy (which I wrote about extensively in my book *Nobel Neo-colonialism*) is spiraling downward as well as alienating former staunch U.S. allies. Regardless of what one says about President Duterte, the vast majority of Filipinos see Mr. Duterte's passionate outbursts, however crude and impolitic, as a strong and fearlessness leader willing to take the actions required to back up his words and provide for his citizenry, no matter how crude, abhorrent and inappropriate other perceive them to be. Too bad we cannot say the same about Obama.

How Obama Fcked Up Yemen

Hard to believe that on October 9, 2009 it was announced that the recipient of that year's Nobel Peace prize would be President Barack Obama for of all things, his promotion of a "new climate" in international relations, especially in reaching out to the Middle East and Muslim world. In December he accepted the award and gave the world a lecture on war and peace with introducing what he referred to as the concept of "just war."

This was in my perception a glance into the future, one in which Obama's peace prize was more a portent of the actions the likes of Henry Kissinger, Theodore Roosevelt, Charles G. Dawes, and Woodrow Wilson than Linus Pauling, Mother Teresa, Nelson Mandela or Martin Luther King, Jr. What has been observed is that since this date, President Obama has been as bellicose if not more so than any president we have had in the modern era. Personally between he, Teddy Roosevelt and Wilson it is likely a tie.

Since then, the Obama Administration has re-introduced a U.S. foreign policy of manifest destiny under the guise of humanitarian intervention. His foreign policy of the "Just war" has put us in and/or extended us in to too many nations to count including but not limited to Iraq, Afghanistan, Syria, Libya, Somalia, Mali, Egypt and Yemen. The last is his most recent and newly deadly war game activity. The war in Yemen (what the Saudi and U.S. call a military intervention) started in 2015, when Saudi Arabia with the support and assistance of leading a coalition of the United Sates, Egypt, Morocco, Jordan, Sudan, the United Arab Emirates, Kuwait, Qatar and Bahrain decided to play with the civilian population of Yemen in an effort to influence the outcome of a new civil war in the small once divide nation.

Obama's policy in Yemen is par for the course. Not only is it directionless and incoherent, it does not have any impact on securing or protecting the interest of the U.S. In 2008, the then senator from Illinois was incessantly complaining about how prior administrations were always messing and sticking their nose in the affairs of other nations, in particular those in the Middle East. It was a period in which Mr. Obama openly indicated his disdain for war, especially proxy wars. Now something has altered and what has arisen is what may be called an Obama Doctrine (the doctrine of Just war). It must be recalled that the current effort in Yemen is the direct result of the people of Yemen overthrowing a U.S. and Saudi-backed and established puppet government in 2014.

In Yemen, as elsewhere Obama has made use of U.S. military might, hardware or personnel for reasons that have no political or pragmatic objective. The President is using his bully pulpit either via advising, troops on the ground, special forces, drones, airstrikes and/or arming select nations as a part of a tool box to fix things he considers broken which in fact were never broken to begin with.

His administration (and the United Kingdom) started its upkeep for the Saudi-led war in Yemen just to show that they had the backs of the Royal House of Saud by basically giving carte blanc to do whatever they want even war crimes. And if this was not bad enough, he just approved a $1.5 billion arms sale to Saudi Arabia, of which includes giving the Saudi's more than 150 M1A2 Abrams battle tanks. Moreover, Obama's backing has not waivered since it began in March 2015. What has come about since then has been the brutal bombing and slaughter of tens of thousands on Yemeni civilians, mostly women and children in what has long been considered the poorest country in the Middle East.

Although Washington relies mostly on Saudi Arabia to do its dirty work, it has its hands equally as deep in the muck. We continue to supply the Saudi with weapons, we also play a significant role in providing intelligence and aerial refueling even while knowing the Saudi's continue (in spite of international law) to unlawfully committee war crimes by bombing hospitals, schools, mosque, weddings and funerals among other sites. Now it has been determined the Obama administration is also supplying Saudi Arabia with white phosphorus which can maim and kill by burning to the bone. It is estimated that tens of thousands of civilians have been killed or wounded thus far and national infrastructure critically damaged or destroyed completely. We have even employed special operations teams on the ground. What I find peculiar is that here we are fighting through direct assistance or proxies, against Houthis from the North, who practice a type of Shia Islam called Zaydi, who we know are at odds and been battling our KNOWN enemy - Al-Qaeda in the Arabian Peninsula (AQAP). And why, well to install a President who ran unopposed, yet still considered legitimate by the Saudi's and Obama administration when Obama personally said that the Burundi elections were "not credible" when President Pierre Nkurunziza won a third term unopposed.

What makes this entire even stranger is that the Yemeni President Abd-Rabbu Mansour Hadi is a known affiliate of the Muslim Brotherhood. The Muslim Brotherhood were instrumental in starting the protests that demanded an end to Ali Abdullah Saleh's three decade rule which in December 2011 resulted in a unelected national unity cabinet which eventually ended up via phony election placing Abd-Rabbu Mansour Hadi as president. So in essence we have the Houthis whom the Saudi's hate, for taking over Sanaa and running a unelected President out of the country, a president aligned with the Muslim Brotherhood whose leadership is closely linked with Yemen's Salafists, who together with al-Qaeda, have been in open confrontation with the revivalist Zaidy group we call the Houthis. Taking it one step further, if I know that the Muslim Brotherhood's Palestinian offshoot in Gaza is Hamas, then what does that make the Muslim Brotherhood's President Obama and Saudi Salafists are trying to install? I will tell you - a terrorist by definition of the U.S. State Department.

It is a very strange situation President Obama has gotten the U.S. involved in, specifically as he expands on our involvement in the undeclared war in Yemen. If it continues to manifest as it appears, this may be forever a dark cloud over Obama's legacy especially when we compare it to how he admonishes the Russians for their operations in concert with Syria in their fight against ISIS. Inordinate human rights organizations including the U.N. and Human Rights Watch has been very critical of the Obama administration and Saudi Arabia for the carnage occurring in Yemen. President Obama is basically allowing for the destruction and murder of tens of thousands of civilians in Yemen and if this is so, the query remains if the broader U.S. policy goal in the country is really stability? For even the novice this cannot be the objective seeing present wide-ranging support for the Saudi's is a clear incongruity with his rhetoric when he suggested it was the U.S. and world's role to stop proxy wars in the Middle East.

For the pragmatic, Yemen cannot be considered as one of Obama's foreign policy success stories, unless his foreign policy legacy is that his actions (or lack of action) has caused millions of Yemenis to exist on the brink of starvation and disease while we assisted their Yemen's more affluent Saudi neighbors smashup a nation just because they wanted to pick on someone.

Does anyone else find this comical and sickening? Just two years ago Obama was all out everywhere giving speeches and making statements to the effect that the war on terror in Yemen was proving to be a great success, with here a drone, there a drone, and everywhere a drone-drone. Yemen is not success and rather an example of feckless foreign policy and mission creep in the form of "I'm just gone do some shit and don't have any idea or don't give a fck about what happens after I start some shit foreign policy." What does he care, He's just gone give the Saudi's cluster bombs and out the other side of his neck complain that Syria is using cluster (barrel) bombs too. So what if they have been banned under the guidance of international war, Obama has no problems if the Saudi's commit war crimes with more than forty percent of their air strikes in Yemen since the bombing campaign began targeting civilians – just as long as it isn't Assad or Putin it is all good. Just this past week Sunni-dominated government (if you can call it that) in Yemen suspended peace talks with the Houthi rebels, because the Houthi demanded a new government that would include them in the governance of the country in which they live. However this was unacceptable to both Saudi Arabia and the United States. So far, the UN says that upwards of 7 million Yemeni are on the verge of starvation with more than seventy percent existing without access to safe drinking water. This folk is the Obama Doctrine - the doctrine of the just war and this is in my purview, why I say Obama done fcked up Yemen.

The Federal Reserve and Income Inequality: Currency and Money Isn't the Same Thing

No one with the singular exception of Donald Trump has even mentioned the Federal Reserve since the start of the primaries through the general election. Sure Hillary Clinton has mentioned income inequality but one cannot have an honest discussion on income inequality without noting that the biggest contributor to wealth inequality the world and America in particular is the U.S. Federal Reserve Banking system – which for the record is no more federal than Federal Express, CVS or the GAP. Anyone who reads and has the math comprehension equal to or above a sixth grade level understands this but cats that watch television and claim to be woke do not.

The Federal Reserve Bank is frankly the biggest scam in the history of the world and by default probably the most crooked institution that has ever existed next to the Church of Scientology. First it is entirely privately owned although it wants the world to see it as or on equal footing to a governmental agency/institution and it has the right to print and issue money just like kings did some 300 plus years ago. But the worse thing about it outside of its money making Ponzi schemes in my opinion is that it exist as a money monopoly seeing it alone has the power over all the money and credit of the people in the United States and frequently beyond. Since its inception (which I hope to discuss in a bit more detail in a few paragraphs to come) what is clear is that the U.S. government had no debt when the Federal Reserve Act was passed in 1913. What may be more astonishing is that it is as I noted previously, a private entity with stock which is not traded openly and no one except the elite of the elite can own only through inheritance singularly.

Through the actions of the Federal Reserve Bank and U.S. treasury, it is no wonder they have the majority of U.S. citizens using the words "currency" and "money" interchangeably when they are not the same thing. First, money is a store of value and has the ability to maintain its value in the form of purchasing power for a very, very long period of time. Money is durable (meaning it never changes over time and it is fungible (meaning it is the same no matter where you are also interchangeable). Money traditionally has been some commodity such as gold, silver or land. Money is created, not printed.

On the other hand currency is simply paper. It is paper money used a tool for trading your time and labor and although it too is fungible and a medium of exchange, currency has no intrinsic value. It is just an official monetary instrument used in commerce. Currency must be "legal tender," which means the government will accept it in payment for taxes. Currency is NOT money, but merely represents money. And it is printed on paper or minted from metal.

What we spend is currency (base money). It is put into circulation by the Federal Reserve, with the assistance of our banking system via buying and selling of securities (mostly bonds). As the money Gods, the Federal Reserve can control the amount of loot in the U.S. economy and at the same time; give loans on money that don't exist just by adding a few zeros to the books and boom – profit making Ponzi. It's called base money because it is the money deposited by the customer, by which money generated through fractional reserve banking is created from.

The main problem with currency is that the Federal Reserve can print more and more of it whenever they want.

Each time they do, it just results in more currency flooded into circulation. Each time they want or need to do this, the more currency added into global circulation, the less value said currency has because the more of it there is the less valuable it becomes. And each time this happens, whether through selling IOUs in the form of Bonds to banks or quantitative easing, the Federal Reserve is unremittingly taking loot out of your pocket directly to the government and their pockets (banks).

Why is this you may ask, well since the Federal Reserve Act was signed by President Wilson on December 23, 1913, today, what we call money and or consider our base currency is really just a receipt – an IOU on a government created and traded bond. How can this be? Well to begin with, when you deposit your loot in a bank, you are not putting it in an account of your own for safe keeping. Instead you are loaning the bank your currency which means they can do whatever they want with it once you do. If the banks want to take your money and gamble with it on the stock, ETF or commodity markets, they can, or if they desire (which is more often the case), they will likely loan it out. And not just loan it out, but loan it out with interest, which is a profit for them through what they call fractional reserve lending.

Through this mechanism, banks are allowed to lend what they don't own and even what they don't even possess ten to twenty times over. In simple terms, Fractional reserve lending is the process whereby banks make up currency by adding zeros to computers and lend that created money that doesn't even exist to make a profit. Fractional reserve banking is the ultimate hustle and exists to drain the common laborer of all their work without paying them for it. See, when a bank accepts your deposit, they give out loans, the loans become another deposit, which becomes another loan, and this cycle repeats itself in perpetuity. And when banks do this, they don't ask us if they can or tell us that are going to do this. Look at it this way, if was a bank, and was required to keep only $1 of the $10 you deposited with me, and loaned the other $9 out, and charged X interest on the loan, but only have only how ca make a profit of plus $10 when there is only 10$ that exist to start with? This is in essence "fractional-reserve" banking (for every $1 the Federal Reserve bank prints the banking system created an additional $9 out of nowhere which equals fraud.

Gone are the days of a family being able to live off of a single pay check. In the past our paper money was just a claim check. It was just a paper representation of real money that you could take to a bank and claim for gold or silver (gold and silver being real money of intrinsic value). The way, in which the U.S. Treasury and Federal Reserve banks operate in concert, the reality is that what they call currency today isn't even paper money, but rather a claim check. To understand this you have to understand the way banks turn deposits into loans and understand how Federal Reserve Bank policies affect the supply of money in general. This entire scheme is called fractional reserve lending and/or banking.

The Federal Reserve Bank is the main culprit of income inequality. Constantly the prices we pay for stuff is soaked up by the Federal Reserve like a sponge because our currency supply is forever growing and expanding. Thus the more currency the more prices will keep on going up which leads to inflation (all because the treasury and Banks swap IOUs in the form of bonds on behalf of the Federal Reserve Bank). And even worse is that this circle continues because the money they get from us in the form of taxes is used to pay interest on IOUs carried by bonds; meaning there is always more debt in our system than currency in circulation to pay the debt.

We need to wake up and understand the difference between currency and money and pay real close attention to the practices of the Federal Reserve Bank, for they don't serve nor care about us, we the people.

Hillary Clinton is Jacob Zuma Twice Over

With this strange period in which political dysfunction it appears cannot get any bizarre or hail maryish on the last play of the game with three seconds left type of ish, I have decide to entertain myself thinking about other things that happen to cross my mind when I tune out. One is what I will address now, how Hillary Clinton reminds me of Jacob Zuma but only two times as worse. Hillary Clinton and Jacob Zuma are the epitome of establishment politics and poster children of what to expect when one uses the system to enrich themselves above and beyond unscrupulous reproach and corruption.

It is easy when you speak of Jacob Zuma, the current President of South Africa to see the level of alleged corruption he is involved. Unlike Hillary he either doesn't care if he is seen as being corrupt, or just sees his job as an avenue for personal profit and such is expected. This is the problem, having lived in South Africa, I know that this is politics as usual. But Zuma had a different orientation into formal governmental politics that just disallowed me to see him, once obtaining office, to be as corrupt as other African politicians after independence.

Zuma was one of the first ANC leaders to return to South Africa to begin the process of negotiations after the ban on the ANC in February 1990. Eventually he would become Deputy President of the ANC, a position which he would be removed from by then ANC President Thabo Mbek in 2005 – due to allegations of corruption and fraud related to a 1999 $5-billion weapons acquisition deal that he profited from economically. Through all of this, Zuma still managed to become the ANC candidate for President in 2009 and was sworn in as President of South Africa that same year and re-elected again in 2014. Being from the ANC, the party of liberty and freedom it just surprised me that he was able to Phi Beta Kappa his corruption skills so quickly.

But Zuma has nothing on Hillary R. Clinton, the present democratic nominee for the U.S. Presidency. HRC has been preparing for this since her Goldwater girl Nixon days. Yes, ever since she was a young lawyer working on the Watergate investigation until her Benghazi testimony, plane to see she has dreamed of this right here – being President of the U.S. Indeed interesting because while with Nixon, she was accused of being unethical during the House Judiciary impeachment inquiry into Watergate – something about lying and hiding some documents.

Likewise multiple investigations made into South Africa's President Jacob Zuma has found evidence of corruption in his administration starting with him. From improper relationships with wealthy businessmen to rape, Zuma's past decade has seen one racketeering charged followed by another, with Zuma repeatedly denying doing anything wrong or unethical. Even in light of evidence that he approved the use of state companies to make himself wealthy.

Hillary Clinton is the valedictorian of using the state and/or the machinery of the state as a vehicle for self-profiteering. From allegedly stealing antiques from the Whitehouse to Travelgate and the death of Vince Foster, from Norman Hsu to her dealings with the King of Morocco or the Russian Rosatom Uranium mine deal; her path was with the added advantage of being white and middle class whereas Zuma was not. Consequently the range and diversity of scandals and allegations collected by the Clintons led them to view white privilege profiteering based on using the state as normal behavior.

And the private server bit – saying you intended to set up the server but you didn't intend to use the server for official state department business. This is harder to understand that her saying she didn't make loot from the Clinton foundation, or that she didn't integrate foundation business with state department business. Hillary has a few bodies too, but I would not put it past Zuma to have some as well. Even still, Hillary has him beat, and just wait to see her expand that lead if she becomes president.

Hillary Clinton: More like Agnew than Obama

Before the resignation of Richard M. Nixon as president of the United States, Spiro Agnew became the first U.S. vice president to resign discredited in scandal. On that very same day, he pleaded no contest to a charge of federal income tax evasion in order to avoid being brought up on charges of political corruption. He got off lightly, just a $10,000 fine, three years' probation, and being disbarred by the Maryland court of appeals.

Agnew, a Republican, was governor of Maryland until he was nominated for the Republican vice presidential candidate in 1968. During 1972-73 the U.S. Justice Department uncovered extensive evidence of political corruption on behalf of Agnew, including the acceptance of bribes even while serving as vice president of the U.S. Lyndon Johnson described Agnew as a person who "became a political celebrity for reasons that had nothing much to do with character or capacity."

HRC has Agnew by a country mile. Just starting over the past few weeks: Abedin telling the FBI the she told the Whitehouse every time Clinton changed emails, HRC's staff removing "top secret" classification markings off emails on her private server (possibly two felonies according to some) the most problematic being felony by possessing and storing top secret information on an insecure server, and "bribes disguised as charitable contributions."

The latter maybe the most nefarious. Agnew was only taking bribes from U.S. corporate interest not foreign governments as is the case with HRC. This encompasses Algeria giving half a million dollars to the Clinton foundation while at the same time lobbying the HRC State Department for special favors and without the approval of the Obama administration. To put it simply, HRC has five FBI investigations (two open investigations), the Weiner pedophilia investigation, as well as the pay-to-play with the Clinton Foundation, and having her email investigation reopened.

I am saying this because it is often projected that HRC is a lot like Obama. Certainly she has some economic and progressive views on big ticket items like the president on guns, health care and regime change, but in disposition and historical attribute, she has more in common with former vice president and governor of Maryland Spiro Agnew.

The way I see it, the academic elitism of HRC prohibits any similarity with Obama. I would speculate that her relationship with Obama will forever change if she is indicted or eventually convicted, their relationship won't end up the same way. After Agnew's resignation in October 1973, he and Nixon never spoke again.

Playing the Markets on the Trump Effect

Over the past week I have noticed many big speculators of the Wall Street ilk expressing, via their monetary and personal wealth actions, that if Trump wins the general elections that they think the market will tank. It was cool for a while with everyone thinking Hillary had this election in the bag but recently it appears the fear that Donald Trump could win has set in on Wall Street. Some of the experts say that a Trump victory would most definitely reduce the value of the S&P 500 and other global stock markets by 10-15%. Given this, it wouldn't surprise me if the largest panic attack is occurring in the equity market arena.

Seems major global financial institutions are afraid of what an unscripted President Trump would do. Would he tear up trade agreements? What would that do to world markets? Will our trade partners cause a trade war as a retaliatory action? What we do know, based on his position papers is that a Trump presidency would likely mean a major tax code transformation, the ending or renegotiation of NAFTA and taxing hedge funds, among other things.

The first sign for me was the dollar. The dollar has been slipping to yen and the euro been slowly moving up. The dollar has also added to the Mexican Peso. While at the same time, we see bond yields going down along with stocks. Even before this, all the chatter should have given warnings of such with so much attention being placed on interest rates and inflation. Around the globe, the feeling is that a rise in inflation is on the way. Warnings of bond market inflation have been uttered from Germany to Canada. If this true then our currency will purchase less and prices will be going higher and higher.

This is what I have to say, just because the markets panic, you should not. When that piercing immediate sell-off on the markets that is bound to happen if Trump wins according to the mainstream (see Brexit) then jump in and buy, buy, buy if you got any spare loot. What I anticipate is that we will see and experience what we observed after Brexit. The market will go through a massive panic sell-off due to perceived future uncertainty and eventually bounce back. We saw this with the Brexit vote when the pound dropped sharply after the vote to leave the EU. Now some months later we see the pound jumping to an almost one-month high against the dollar. In fact the same experts are outing a similar outcome with a Trump Victory as they did with a Brexit vote – that if fully implemented, Trump's economic policies will result in a loss of anywhere between 4 and 11 million U.S. jobs. The main stream media is serving as an echo chamber for these sentiments.

Even before Brexit, when the first steps towards a European currency were taking place in 1972 history saw the Sterling drop out after only six weeks, weaker than ever, bowing to the dictates of the markets. In 1976 we saw the pound fall below $2 for the first time but eventually the Sterling proved too strong. What will likely happen, is that Central banks around the world will intervene to keep whatever currency that is on top from becoming too strong. Martin Weitzman in his 2007 paper *Subjective Expectations and Asset-Return Puzzles*, noted that most of the time such economic disasters (like a 10-15%) drop on a given index like S&P) did not occur. Although it is possible theoretically that the S&P could fall by X percent for any given number of months, in economic reality you are sure to lose loot in the short-term, but eventually your expected upside will always be greater. Even if inflation runs well above its target or above short term bond/stock yields.

Mosul: A Game of Risk

Once upon a time before this age of video games, cell phones and 24 hour continuous cable television, there were four television stations and they all went off around midnight to a hollow vapid medium pitch tone with the picture of an Indian in the background. This was a period in which if you were not outside playing and being active, if you were inside and not reading you were playing a game with your family of friends. Typically this was either in cards but mainly board games. One such board game which was one of my favorites was Risk. Made by Parker Brothers, Risk is a strategy board game that has three main objectives: to control entire continents to get reinforcement armies, to protect and watch ones borders and to protect and defend against other neighboring armies/nations that could attack you and building up ones military on their own borders for defensive purposes.

It was a heated game and brought the best and worst out in most people whom played it, with each player accumulating and stacking up those little squares in anticipation of a possible impending attack. In Risk, a player has the best chance of winning if the hold continents since this is the best way to increase reinforcements. Players often attempt to gain control of Australia early in the game, since Australia is the only continent that can be successfully defended via heavy fortification (continents with fewer borders are easier to defend).

The battle for Mosul is on after Obama announcing out loud it would be eventually taking place before the end of 2016. The way I am seeing this adventure in Mosul is just like a game of Risk. To take the city you have to first get past all of the villages on the outskirts of the city. Imagine having to go through Newnan or Smyrna, Georgia to get to Atlanta. But in this city, every road like Peachtree Street has IEDs buried all through them and on every roof there is a sniper. If you manage to get through this, in the back of your mind you know that the cats that have been there have been dug in for two years and that they have the advantage.

The West of Mosul is the old city and from what I have been told, it will be difficult for anyone to go in and fight there – can't drive Humvees or tanks because the roads are too tight and thin and ISIS is going to put a stiff front against the U.S.- Iraqi coalition forces as they enter.

This doesn't even include considering the post conflict environment in Mosul, which will be a very difficult path itself to navigate. I mean, you can't remove 1.5 million Mosul residents for a few thousand ISIS militants and we can't make the same mistakes we did by allowing Iraqi security forces to completely demolish everything in sight as we did in Fallujah, Ramadi or Tikrit (or it will set the same conditions that allowed ISIS to grow in the first place), unless it is the Obama Administration goal to push ISIS west into Syria. The danger of this however is that it will take a very long time to get ISIS out of Mosul and the civilians will suffer disproportionately.

How Mosul will be governed after or if ISIS leaves is another query. Has the Obama team thought about it – a city predominantly Sunni and Iraqi security forces predominately Shia? This will be a very extremely complicated task for we will approach this act as if it is a typical Western intervention and a typical Arab city. Unfortunately Mosul isn't your average Arab city. It is a very multi-cultural city centered between Syria and Turkey. It is a very diverse city filled with Sunni, Shiite, Kurds and Christians. Taking one bank of the Tigris River will be easy, but to take the entire city, will be something that will take a long time. Which reminds me again, what the after plan is if and/or after Mosul falls? How will the US coalition deal with a large Iraqi Force, a large Kurdish force and the desire that Shia militia have to get in on the action? All which are paramount issues that worry the Turks (Sunni), who are as we speak training anti-ISIS fighters in the strategic town of Bashiqa and want to enter Mosul and engage in battle. They are vehemently against Shia militias taking part in any fighting in the city; for Erdogan has openly said he thinks Mosul should be a city for Sunni Turkmen, Sunni Kurds and Sunni Arabs.

Turkey already has troops in Iraq and they are not welcomed nor were invited by the Iraqi government. They are not very diplomatic because they claim that Mosul is a Turkish city while at the same time Kurds want autonomy in Iraq, especially Mosul and display even stronger and similar feelings as it pertains to in Northern Iraq.

Turkish military is also training Sunni tribes with the hope of keeping a migration from Mosul to Turkey from occurring. The Peshmerga (Kurds) are coming in from the east heading west to make sure they keep folk from going to Kurdistan and Shia militias are on the West to keep ISIS from going into Syria. Yes, this is a big old game of Risk.

And what of the U.S.? Well after getting rid of Saddam Hussein, they city still lacks consistent running water and consistent electricity due to the U.S. invasion as is the case for most of Iraq and the anti U.S. animosity remains high. For many Iraqis, the U.S. has not only failed to make life better than it was under Saddam Hussein, it has made daily living worse. Strangely, before ISIS took root in Mosul, it was touted as being more secure than Baghdad. Presently, ISIS has every vehicle, building, child, cat and dog rigged with explosives and if success is to be had in Mosul, it will be a street by street, neighborhood by neighborhood, house by house dog fight.

If America continues on this path of the feckless Obama-Clinton – Bush-Rumsfeld foreign policy approach, President Obama could be leaving his predecessor another Aleppo. Not only is the Iraqi government corrupt as all get out, none of the cats doing the fighting trust each other (U.S. military, Kurdish Peshmerga, Turks or Shia militias).

In all honesty, if Mosul is liberated, it will be the start of a bigger war and an excuse for the Obama administration to move into Syria which I believe is his true desire albeit we ALL know Washington hasn't planned properly nor is ready for such an event (See Libya and Yemen). I may be wrong, but you tell me if the present administration, like the prior, has outlined any strategic goals or objectives for achieving such and dealing with the aftermath other than aerial bombardments? And if I am correct, it will be more wasting of the loot of the American people when our problems should be first and foremost on the table for solution finding regarding our struggling economy.

Mosul is problematic. Not only is there no central command, without the U.S., Kurds and Shia militias, the Iraqi Security Forces would never be able to take the city on their own and would probably run as they did when ISIS first entered Iraq. Add this to the tangible hatred between all involved, it would be highly unlikely for everybody, in particular when you throw the Turks in the mix, not to just end up shooting at each other. Even if this doesn't manifest, what is consistent is that it will represent regardless of the outcome, more failed U.S. foreign policy and more dead bodies and destroyed communities since our only answer is to just give out weapons to whoever we decide to support, not based on logic nor the interest of the people living in the Middle east

And you can best believe if Hillary Clinton becomes the president elect, the D.C. neocon and neoliberal foreign policy establishment will be salivating for more U.S. intervention which would probably be in the form of a no-fly zone, that would not save anyone or help the people on the ground or get rid of ISIS, but rather cause more problems and maybe even a direct confrontation with Syria, Russia and Iran. But if I were optimist I would speculate that, we may get rid of ISIL in Mosul, eventually, but what will come next after them to fill the void is my concern.

Four Wars and Counting

I am very well aware that there are so many conflicts occurring that it is hard to keep track of them all. This new world era of geopolitical hegemony is tricky. Yet still, of all of the conflicts I am having a problem taking my eyes off of India and Pakistan. Tensions between New Delhi and Islamabad have been running high ever since India cracked down on protests in Indian-administered Kashmir in July.

Over the past month there have been several events that make this situation both interesting and frighten. There was an assault that occurred in Kashmir on sept 18 in which four gunmen took an Indian army brigade headquarters in the Indian controlled town of Uri which resulted in the death of 18 soldiers. Although no one claimed responsibility for the attack, the government of Prime Minister Narendra Modi's accused Pakistan and even called it a terrorist state for supporting the individuals Modi believed were behind the attack. The Modi administration purports that the attack was carried out by members of Jadish-e-Mohammed (a group based in Pakistan that has the aim of forcing the withdrawal of troops in India-controlled Kashmir). More recently, an Indian army brigade headquarters near the de factor border with Pakistan was attacked which left 17 soldiers dead in the northern region of Kashmir.

Then on the 21st of October, seven Pakistani Rangers were killed and three others injured when the Border Security Force (BSF) of India retaliated shelled and fired from across the International Border at locations near and around the Kathua and Jammu districts of Kashmir. The only information that has been proffered is that Islamabad has rejected all allegations made by New Delhi's in an effort to take attention away from human rights violations in Indian-controlled Kashmir, while Pakistan has asserted that the Indian Army is just firing at citizens and military outpost without provocation.

Whatever the case and whoever fired first, this is getting in dangerous territory. From what I have read, there have been at least four wars between India and Pakistan, if not more if I included other minor skirmishes. The first happened in 1947. This was called by many as the First Indo-Pakistani War. Like most wars it stated over some dumb shit – the belief that the royal leader of Kashmir would pledge his nation's allegiance to India. He had the choice to join India or Pakistan or to remain independent. The problem was that he was a Hindu and ruled a majority Muslim population and this was a no-no for Pakistan, so they attacked and occupied parts of Kashmir and this was the first war. It took UN Security Council involvement for a formal cease-fire to occur and on New year's eve 1949, India gained control of about two-third of Kashmir and Pakistan a third. The second war occurred in 1965 after Pakistan's military joined with militants from Jammu and Kashmir to start an insurgency against Indian rule in the region. This resulted in India launching a full-scale military attack on what was then West Pakistan. Although it only lasted for a week, the 1965 Indo-Pakistani War resulted in thousands of casualties and was considered by some historians to have been the largest tank battle since World War II. The war only ended after the Soviet Union and USA got involved to negotiate a truce between Islamabad and New Delhi. Believe it or not, the same thing happened again in 1971 and 1991.

The new region at issue is the border along the Himalayan River. Just this week seven civilians, including two minors, were killed and several others wounded when Pakistani troops shelled several districts along the border. This was not the first time Pakistani troops have shelled the area or broken the ceasefire. It has been reported that India Border Security Force destroyed fourteen Pakistani posts when they responded with heavy mortar fire.

It seems that almost daily we are getting information regarding either one side shooting or shelling the other side. Most recently involved Pakistani officials say Indian troops have opened fire across the Line of Control in the disputed region regularly and they continue to respond with heavy fire as a consequence.

I cannot imagine either side wanting a war. The major issue for me is that both are nuclear powers – yes, both have the bomb(s). On bare equipment, I would think that Pakistan wouldn't even want to engage India in a war. India has a clearly larger military and more money. Many around the globe consider India's economy as being more stable than its neighbor and one of the fastest growing economies in the world in the last decade. India also has several other advantages: India has a population of 1.2 Billion compared to 199 million for Pakistan; India has military aircraft – more than two thousand compared to less than a thousand for Pakistan and Indian spends around forty billion annually on its military compared to around seven billion for Pakistan.

Likewise, India has enough problems on its hands after this past summer and its violent and bloody response to protest by the oppressed citizens of Kashmir, ever since military and police killed a young leader sparked uprisings across the Kashmir region which has resulted in the deaths of around a hundred people, leaving hundreds of other blinded. By some estimates, over the past several months almost twenty thousand (adults and children) have been injured, and several thousand placed under arrest spending and living the past months under curfews in Kashmir.

With all of the violence presently happening in the world, especially in the region many call the Middle East, it is extremely important that we keep an eye on this, for history has shown us the region of Kashmir is a hotbed and its people crave independence away from India at any cost. In addition, it doesn't take much for Islamabad and New Delhi to go to war with each other, and maybe even making use of the nuclear option. There have already been four significant wars between the two nations over the past seventy years, I just wonder if we may be seeing the start of the fifth.

Clinton versus Trump
Was Dewey versus Truman on Steroids

It is obvious that a sizeable corpus of US citizens are still walking around in a daze, shell shocked for lack of a better phrase after the stunning (for some) upset defeat of the Hillary Clinton and DNC campaign machine to novice Donald Trump for the presidency of the United States of America. Not me, in fact I expected such.

Sure, this was an anti-beltway, anti-establishment and anti-elite election outcome, but even more so, it was against corporatism. I know many may find this a difficult assertion to understand, and will say "but Trump is a billionaire" – and you are correct. However being a billionaire isn't the same as being a corporatist. Trump made his money in real estate via a private company, not through hedge funds, big banks, or Wall Street financial institutions. These are corporations, therefore he is not beholden to the strings that come with having to depend on them for money in any form or fashion as a Hillary Clinton and most House members regardless of party affiliation.

See folk whom were surprised and even upset are removed, far removed from the daily activity associated with the lives of average Americans, in particular those that don't regular frequent Starbucks or shop at Wholefoods, don't use Uber and who live in country and rural areas. They don't know what it is like to chop down a tree on their property and pull out the chainsaw and sell a couple of cords for a little pocket change, or for whom going out mean eating at Waffle House or buying Barbque from the black dude parked on the side of the road with a big grill on the back of his F-150. These the cats that voted for Trump. If my small town of 2300 is an example, I can speak for a fact that these folk ain't racist, bigots or intolerant. They are Black, White,

Asian, Latino and Hispanics. In fact everyone in my town, White, Black, Asian or Hispanic were pro-Trump and proud.

They are straight talking people with no pomp or circumstance. They don't get turned off by words for actions speak louder. They are not hypocrites: unlike the cats whom hold disdain for Trump's perceived misogynistic statements but be up in the club or be bumping the misogyny of Lil Wayne, Drake or Jay-Z and knowing, as well as singing along with each word, if not shaking they azz in the club and don't even include shake booty joints. Yes, this election was about the rural versus urban, country versus city divide equally.

The mainstream media and press have been dealing with Hillary so long she was basically consider as one of their own – one of them. There is a different set of values imbued in people who do their own plumbing when there is a leaky pipe, change their own oil on their truck and do their own dry walling when they need to patch a hole in a wall when compared to people that typically do not know how to do or take care of themselves in such a manner.

This is what pollsters have either avoided or forgotten about. When you sample mostly city and urban areas, these type of people are lost in the mix and you will have more college-educated people in your sample albeit they may not be representative of the population of "likely voters" which means you have zero external validity. This is the main reason why it is often disremembered that polls are not and can never be scientific because they are not systematic. There is no systematic standard for any poll. Having your temperature or blood pressure taken is a systematic process because the standard method of calibration remains the same regardless of time. Unlike this, polls base their standards on prior elections which are always changing and included different proportions based on who voted in the past – this is neither scientific nor systematic. Most pollsters and statistical models gave Hillary Clinton's chances of winning more than 90%. This was true all over – especially for Pennsylvania, Wisconsin, and Michigan. What happened is that these folk oversampled and adjusted their polls to give them the result they wanted instead of the result that would be true. This is not scientific for it is not objective.

But such reflects the frowzy dispositions of inherent bias and isolation proffered by urban city dwellers. See, cats like us are seen by them as living in the places they fly over going form New York City to Miami or Portland to Chicago. They look down from 35,000 feet and just see land, not people – this is how out of touch they are. For them, we are just cats to mock, laugh at, call ignorant and backwards. This is modern journalism and political punditry at its best – smug and contemptuous for much of the electorate because it is easier to call folk names like racists and sexists as opposed to get to know them. Why, because it is easier to think for us because they are smarter and know better. THIS is true bigotry. We ain't followers the way mainstream elite desire for us to be, we not the kind of folk that shut up and get in line because we are told too (See President Obama as Example number one).

For me it is not the name calling that is the worse part, it is the fact that inside the belt way and other city like folk in the media and politics don't even try, or make an effort to really try and understand folk like us. Facts are only facts when they spout them even when absent of reason and logic. For example, the folk the media and punditry class are calling Trump supporters racist although they are the same Wisconsin, Michigan and Pennsylvania voters who supported Obama in 2008. Many were the same who supported Sander's over Clinton as well. Were they racist, sexist and bigots when they supported him?

Time for city cats to wake up. There is no post truth era. The truth is (unlike those giving the analysis) that the majority of Americans ain't making six figures a year let alone getting six figures to give a speech for 30 minutes. They are the seventy plus percent of households making less than $60,000 a year. So GET OUT OF YOUR FEELINGS, stop whining and crying. Man up and don't be such a puzzy you act as if this is a shock when it wasn't. It were you city folk that decided to poll each other (mostly college educated folk). So deal with it, you haters were on our bodies, so we shook you off.

Assad, Trump, Putin and Rethinking Syria

With sixty-five days remaining before President Elect Donald Trump takes office, one of the more pressing foreign policy concerns, even from his mouth involves ISIS and Syria. In particular given the international disquiet and precarious uncertainty member states of the European Union have displayed before and after his election.

Prior to the U.S. completion of the primary election, the EU and Obama administration were not completely inagreement on how to address Syria or ISIS. On the one hand the Obama Administration only claim of success was the destruction of Assad's chemical weapons capability, which was achieved mainly because of the influence of Russia. However, outside of this, the Obama administration has been unable to contain the Syrian crisis and has resulted in a mass exodus of refugees into surrounding nation and Europe.

Consequently the EU is just as confused as the present administration and is all over the place with respect to any consistent policy options pertaining to Syria as one would expect with 28 different member states. Instead of embracing Putin, the EU adopted the position of President Obama from 2011 and the leaders of some of the nations, including Prime Minister David Cameron of Britain, President Nicolas Sarkozy of France and Chancellor Angela Merkel of Germany repeated verbatim that Assad must go.

Instead of working with Putin to attempt to destroy a common foe, the Obama administration has resulted to the childish action of name calling as opposed to formulating a geopolitical policy to address ISIS. In one such instance, Samantha Power, US ambassador to the UN accused Russia of supporting "barbarism" upon which she and representatives to the UN from the UK and France walked out right when the Syrian representative was to address the council. Even when Obama decided to work with Putin concerning a ceasefire in Aleppo, he was unable to bring fellow NATO member Turkey along, who believes that such would end in a redrawing of the battlefield of Syria in favor of Bashar Assad's regime and the Kurd's.

Beyond the Islamic State group and al-Qaida, the citizens of the EU are more concerned with the massive influx of immigrants and a succession of terror attacks in France, Belgium and Germany more than Assad. Trump's approach is more in line with the citizens of the EU and US than the leadership of the US and EU independent nations.

Trump's election will obviously take U.S. Syrian foreign policy in a direction in contrast to the EU and President Obama. His approach seems to be more political and diplomatic including working with Putin and Assad if his views on regime change are sincere. Trump has said the U.S. will close its borders to refugees from the Syrian civil war which is in diametric opposition to the stance taken by Merkel. It is also understood from his statements made during the second presidential debate that his focus would be on defeating the Islamic State as opposed to going against Russia or Assad, or seeking regime change in Syria.

He has also openly stated he viewed Putin as a good leader and a person he could work with looking for peace and cooperation as opposed to war and animosity. Similarly, he has offered a not too positive picture of the Saudi's and NATO. One reason for this is that during the republican primary and general election Trump placed domestic policy as his most unyielding concern.

Just this past week Trump indicated that he would stop supplying weapons to anti-Assad forces on the ground. This is consistent with some of his past statements in which he has been quoted as saying "My attitude was you're fighting Syria, Syria is fighting ISIS, and you have to get rid of ISIS. Russia is now totally aligned withSyria, and now you have Iran, which is becoming powerful, because of us, isaligned with Syria... Now we're backing rebels against Syria, and we have noidea who these people are." He has even warned that if the US attacks Assad, "we end up fighting Russia, fighting Syria."

All of this is speculation with the exception of the President Elect's words and his media described "isolationism." We still have to wait for him to put together his administration and name a secretary of state. What is certain is that the back and forth that pigeon-holed the Obama Administration, his Department of State, the Pentagon and CIA on ISIS and regime change in Syria are over.

Extortion in 3 Letters is IMF

I am on record saying that one of the biggest scams in the world is the U.S. Federal Reserve bank. Now I am prepared to announce that the biggest hustle in the world is the International Monetary Fund (IMF). From its inception, the IMF has only served as legalized vehicle for extortion. I observed this firsthand the two years I lived in Nigeria from 1992 to 1993. Then the creature of choice was what the IMF called Structural Adjustment Programs. These programs basically gave loans from the IMF (with the World Bank) to nations that were experiencing economic hardship. These programs were supposed to grow the economies of developing nations, by making them more market focused in an effort to increase trade and as a consequence reduce poverty. That was all everyone across Nigeria spoke of, SAP and how it was driving their nation to economic ruin. It was the first time I'd ever heard of the program or really paid attention to the IMF.

In order to qualify for the loans, borrowing nations have to follow a strict guidance provided by the IMF to make sure they will be able to make debt repayments on the older debts owed to international bankers, governments and the IMF/World Bank. The biggest catch is what I refer to as legalized pillaging – the requirement that borrowing countries devalue their currencies against the dollar; lift all regulations and restrictions on imports and exports and establish price control mechanisms. Although these programs have gone by the wayside in name, they still very much exist in practice (See Greece and Egypt).

Established in 1945 as the agency supposed to oversee the Bretton Woods system and encourage economic growth globally, the IMF basically is an international credit union that is supposed to serve the needs of poorer nations around the world. Unfortunately, the vast majority of IMF programs typically increase poverty rates in the country they say they desire to assist. This comes about because most IMF policies end up making less developed and developing third world countries more dependent on wealthier western nations. How is it that this is the case with an organization whose primary mandate is to reduce poverty yet instead makes it worse? Namely through the implementation of policy that transfers control of economic factors to the private sector from the public sector (Neoliberalism). Through neoliberalism, and focusing on pegging currency to the dollar and debt repayment being top priorities of IMF programs, developing countries end up reducing spending on things the need like health, education and infrastructure development.

Let's us look at the recent example of Egypt. The IMF just approved a three-year, more than $11 billion euros bailout program for Egypt aimed at trying to get the nations besieged economy back on a steady foot. But in order to get the loan, Egypt had to take out another loan of more than 5 billion euros from a combination of funds from other banks, China, other G7 countries and via bond issues. More troubling was that the government had to let the Egyptian Pound devalue by almost half and was mandated by the IMF to end subsidies for fuel, introducing a value-added tax to raise revenues and writing new legislation to decrease Egypt's public sector wages. All of this being an incentive for increasing poverty in Egypt with lower wages and higher fuel prices for the average citizen. The hope is the IMF loan will make Egypt more stable, not lead to further unrest (utter hilarity).

We can also look at what happened in Greece in their relationship with the IMF. After the fact we now see the IMF was way out of step with pragmatic economic policy with respect how they handled the economic problems of the nation of Greece as noted in a report conducted by their Independent Evaluation Office (IEO). In Greece, the IMF signed off on a bailout in 2010 itself was not certain it would help to bring country's debts under control or lead to an economic recovery. Still, the IMF did what it usually did – tried to force through an "internal devaluation" via deflationary wage cuts since the Greek economy was on the Euro. The result however was a disaster. Not only did this action shrink the economic base and grow the national debt, it weighed down the Greek citizenry since the objectives of the bailout were to protect the EU-IMF monetary union rather than the nation. Since the introduction of these excruciating economic measures, the Greek economy has been in a depression ever since.

Honestly, the bailouts for Greece, Portugal and Ireland demonstrated the ineptness of the EU, Christine Lagarde and the IMF to the surface for all to see – that they had either no understanding of the seriousness of the problem or lacked a complete understanding of currency theory.

The problem with the IMF in simple terms is that it has the primary aim of extracting wealth from nations suffering during troubling economic times and despair. Moreover, they have no real policy tools (at least currently) to aid in reducing public debt and controlling inflation in a manner that will also guard the country's poor against the ramifications of what happens when debt repayment is the top priority. Until this changes, IMF policies will continue to keep on reducing the people of developing countries and poorer nations to lower standards of living.

The extortion of poorer nations and/or taking advantage of a country in a time of economic desolation is criminal. There are really no other choices when such economic adversity occurs. First, for foreign investment to come in, investors typically ask that regulations be removed that were designed to be safe guards for the people. The impact of such are more often than not even more distressing and frequently end up imparting even more misery for the developing nations as well as keeping them dependent on richer developed nations.

The shake down and exaction game of the IMF is tight too. After taking the loot, the target nation has to export more in order to raise enough money to pay off their debts on time (an IMF loan requirement). Next, the exports or natural resources become even cheaper to purchase to benefit the consumers in the developed countries and not the poorer nation. This mean these nations have to increase exports just to keep their currencies stable, meaning they spend less on the needs of the people, and eventually the value of labor decreases, capital flows become more unpredictable (see Asian financial crisis of 1997 & Tequila banking crisis of 1994) and the probable outcome is social unrest, riots and protests.

Funny thing is that the IMF is still doing the same thing (although not called SAP anymore) and as I noted earlier, the most recent example is with Egypt. Sadly, their feckless policy approach has yet to change and we are certain to see similar outcomes of civil unrest and riots if they continue on this path. I will give Egypt less than two years.

The Beyhive is filled with Simpletons Or Why the Political Acumen of Beyoncé and Jay Z Count for Nothing

I found it thoroughly comical and insulting that during the final stretch of the general election that instead of stating policy specifics, or going around from county to county, Hillary Clinton fell back on staying to large urban cities and using the classic pandering strategy of pulling out entertainers to appeal to that portion of the voting populous that was fond of mindless self-absorbed celebrity twaddle and suckers for the old bread and circus trick. Beyoncé, Jay-Z, Lady Gaga, Big Sean, J. Cole and Chance the Rapper and LeBron James among many other were among the huge out of touch with the real-world stars called out like trained circus animals to publicly perform for blacks and beg for support on their behalf for them to back Hillary Clinton from mainly urban black millennials.

This is the tradition of the democratic party toward blacks: the poorly read black population don't need to be taken seriously, just entertained, nothing more nothing less. She doesn't even care that she brings a Big "Anthony Weiner sexting" Sean out on stage albeit she is accusing trump of objectifying women because she knows and don't care that blacks whom would vote for her because she has Jay-Z and

Beyoncé on stage with her are dumb as fck anyway. Or a Jay-Z, whom with R. Kelley has a song called Pussy.

It is as if the only thing we care about is drooling over famous folks whose lives are far removed from us regular cats. What the DNC and HRC campaigned failed to grasp is that black folk can think and do frequently think for ourselves and have an uncanny ability to see beyond the snake oil. Despite parading all of them tricks in front of young black voters she was unable to convince black voters that we were a monolith, a single mind, or worse that we wanted four more years of the nothing we got from Obama with the exception of Frantz Fanon called *Black Skin, White Mask.*

And since she didn't secure our vote at the same levels of our first Mulatto president, she and the DNC now wish to lay some of the blame on the Black voting block for her election night loss of the presidency. The roots of Donald Trump's shocking, long-shot, and divisively improbable rise to the presidency can be traced back to election night four years ago when black voter percentage, for the first time in American history, surpassed whites. Black voters led the multiracial groups of voters that re-elected Barack Obama and seemed poised to do so for any democrat in the future.

The election of Donald Trump signifies a lot of things but one was a rebuke to popular culture's political influence in general – for if you depending on the black vote to win you already loss, especially with your record which you desire us to ignore. And true city Negroes ignored it, us real ones did not. And I say really because city cats got it twisted. We know how democrats pimp our votes, and sure, we mad when a police officer kills a black man, any black man, even criminals, but we even more upset when our kids die as a result of gang members killing our kids. Point being we know liberal democrats and many cops don't really care about black folk anyway. In one case we just a vote and the other just target practice.

After all, you can't do no more to get the black vote than to entertain them and giving us fish in the form of free shit that makes us dependent on your monkey azz than to assist us in learning to fish and providing for and taking care of ourselves. It should have been an easy task even for a closet racist the likes of Hillary Clinton for all she had to do was play on our ignorance of history and employ the mainstream media to convince us that all of our ills are all due to Republicans (even in cities where they have not been in power 70 years or more). See the Democrats know that regardless of race, if one is ignorant, don't read, uneducated, under-educated and watch TV, propaganda campaigns work every time – even when you have no message or plan but rather only the use of dog whistles (sexist, racist, xenophobic) and name calling you pay millionaires to repeat.

True you may mention some shit about Planned Parenthood even though Margaret Sanger was racist who viewed blacks as inferior and deserved to be a part of her genocide to exterminate blacks and other less desirables via abortion, but that is only catchy for women whom think murdering a child in utero is just another form of birth control, nonetheless, the Democrats remains and will always remain the party of racism and its voters too imprudent to know they're supporting racism each time they cast their votes for democrats. As if black folk can't do anything for ourselves without the democrats – a train of thought eerily similar to the attitudes and beliefs of paternalistic Democrats just scores of years prior when they justified slavery, fought to keep slavery legal, founded the KKK, pushed Jim Crow laws into existence and opposed school segregation and the Civil Rights Act of 1964. And I won't even mention Chicago (but I did) where black folk 12 times more likely to be shot than whites and where Democrats been on control since the 1930s.

Fact is democratic policies have worsen black poverty, which is still twice that of white poverty and has basically destroyed the black family. So yea, I'm certain Beyoncé and Jay Z threw down, but the votes the Democratic Party and HRC got from such was from a group of pusillanimous embarrassing and unctuous hypocritical whining simpletons that actually accurately reflects the political acumen of Beyoncé and Jay Z.

Trump is Correct: TPP isn't a Fair or Free Trade Agreement

Since the democratic and republican primaries, trade has become a central issue mainly due to the rhetoric of Bernie Sanders and Donald Trump. Although Hillary Clinton jumped on the bandwagon, her insincerity did not add much credibility to her position or even inform others on her position to international trade deals in particular the TPP (Trans-Pacific Partnership) and TTIP (Transatlantic Trade and Investment Partnership), given her documented back and forth between supporting and being against the agreements.

I learned of the TPP years ago but only read of its details when portions of the massive 12 nation trade deal was released by WikiLeaks. This was verified by a release of the document by member signee New Zeland some few months later. For some reason, it is considered a good deal and represents all associated with "free trade." Unfortunately, TPP is never discussed in nuance – in respect to free trade versus fair trade. Many feel that since President Elect Donald Trump has vowed to scrap TPP and readdress previous deals such as NAFTA that free trade will take a major hit and will strike a strong blow against US economic prosperity and the average citizen. However in my simple view, this is and will not be the case.

The market the TPP addressed represented 40 percent of the global economy and from reading it, one can reasonably question two pertinent points of order: 1) does it place foreign interest over US interest and 2) does it place global international corporate interest before US corporate interest? In addition, no one seems to ask if the TPP portends significant economic benefits and/or whom are these benefits for? I ask this because now, both Elizabeth Warren and Bernie Sanders and other democrats have reversed course and are saying it would be bad to renegotiate it since Trump plans to table the deal.

For starters in the US, the TPP if implemented will lead to the creation of only a small amountof jobs. In reading the text, it is clear that there are no parameters that mandate or even suggest that the other eleven signees invest in the US but rather that the US and other nations invest in all nations in exclusion of the US. For example, not including the main body of the TPP agreement, it also includes 58 side agreements of which Japan alone enjoys 14 of these. These specifically lay out distinctive conditions for Japan's participation in the TPP for targeted economic sectors they feel are essential for their domestic economic advantage. Is this free trade? Is this fair trade? If it isn't, it supports the contention of what one of the writers of a blog I regularly read when he stated: "free trade is an unwise policy that has a cascade of negative consequences" and that as a policy "inevitably produces poverty and economic instability, not prosperity."

Thus from this purview, this Trans-Pacific Partnership will do nothing in reality to address the dwindling US middle class or increase stagnant wages experienced by the majority of US workers and most likely make their economic condition even worse. To begin with, the nations involved in this deal are not equal and vary in many respects. National wealth, standards of living, wage differences and even currency valuation. In fact most of the TPP doesn't even address trade but rather investment. The most significant parts of the TPP pertain to investment provisions that make it easier and beneficial for US corporations to put more loot in these nations in the form out sourcing jobs and production to these eleven nations more than serving to increase wages for US workers and job growth.

With most of the 25,000 plus categories of exported good, the US exported basically nothing to TPP nations over the past few years which mean US exporters and producers will remain at a virtual disadvantage to the other eleven participant nations.

Then there are wages. Macro and micro economic theory historically has documented that wages are a major part in the cost of producing goods. Karl Marx even wrote a book on this concept. Thus US corporate interest can only reap large profits via an overall decrease in wages by having these products produced in nations in which wages are substantially lower than they are in the US. This means if this is the definition of free trade, it only means a massive transfer of wealth from US workers to nations outside of the US. Thus, the real and only winners will be US transnational corporations and Wall Street. This is even without the consideration of currency manipulation. Since presently the dollar is freely traded in markets as the world's reserve currency, it will never be in a position to compete with member TPP nations since most engage in some form of currency manipulation that give their products an inherent competitive advantage over US goods.

One doesn't have to take my word for it. The Peterson Institute , Economic Research Service report and the World Bank show limited if any benefits from the TPP and indicate that gains (if any) to the US economy will be negligible in regards to GDP. This is even supported by economists at Tufts University, which predict a net GDP loss for the US via TPP. Another study reports that increases in imports from these countries will result in significant job dislocations and wage declines in the U.S. which means US workers will have to settle forlower-quality jobs.

TPP from my analysis will only mean unequal growth for the US economy compared to the other member nations. Sure, the macroeconomic benefits of the deal are unquestioned, but from my point of view the issue should be the microeconomic impact in the US. If I remained honest, the TPP clearly is more about China than trade or economic development in the US the way in which President Obama describes it. For it will only impoverish the US working class even more, resulting in an even more downward trend on wages, meaning US workers would not even be in an economic condition to by these products. To put it as plainly as possible, the more we import, the more US jobs are displaced (see 2012 US–Korea free trade agreement).

What proponents of the TPP (Obama Administration, IMF, World Bank, transnational corporations & Wall Street) forget is that you can't have true free/fair trade without addressing at a minimum currency manipulation and Value Added Taxes (VAT) applied to American exports at the port of entry. But this makes too much sense and common sense in modern economic policy since the Clinton administration has long been thrown out of the window to benefit the top 1% instead of the average US family.

Notes on the Greenspan Culture

Most Americans are ignorant to the history and impact of central bank policy in the US on the problems we are experiencing and have experienced before regarding our economy. The first failure came when Alexander Hamilton introduced the concept of having a Central Bank in America right after the revolutionary war. His idea was to place the US in a positon to be able to get loans or credit from lenders and be able to borrow great sums of money. To get the bank started, he proposal to fund a national debt via several bills in 1790 including the Debt-Assumption and Debt Funding Bills. With this concept would come massive speculation and fractional reserve banking. Many were against this idea. Thomas Jefferson wrote about this when his cousin Chief Justice John Marshall used the views of Hamilton to uphold the constitutionality of a national bank in his McCulloch v Maryland decision, in essence putting the nation on a dependency of credit. Jefferson noted that the constitution had not delegated to the congress to be able to incorporate a bank (10th amendment) nor to borrow or regulate commerce and that the establishment of a national bank was not necessary, merely a convenience and congress had the constitutional duty to do what was necessary only (pps. 502-574).

Failures of Federal Reserve policy since then and over the years have been too numerous to cite. The issue is that the Federal Reserve and the concept of central banks in general act as if they are independent institutions when the truth is they are never independent. This was understood by both Andrew Jackson and FDR, and to a lesser extent Abraham Lincoln. Central banks seem to operate in a vacuum that is isolated from the public and even worse, the public angst and disdain regarding their policy efforts.

Central banks are failing and have been failing for a long time since their most recent establishment under the Woodrow Wilson administration under the cloak of darkness. These chronic problems keep rearing their ugly head because the models that they employ are broken for they fail to connect monetary policy with the real economy (aggregate demand). This has become more problematic since the reign on Alan Greenspan. This Greenspan culture operates on constructs that don't exist in the real world and even seems to suggest central bankers of the current batch have no idea of what is going on in the rest of the world outside of Jackson Hole. No matter what they do it always fails and never accomplishes the goals or objectives that said monetary policy was supposed to accomplish.

Take the example of quantitative easing and keeping interest rates artificially low and constant. This was supposed to put more loot into the coffers of business and to some extent the people and spur consumption - the assumption being that if you give folk more loot they will spend it, or at least consume more. But we see just by looking at consumption behavior, business are not spending by either investing or buying equipment and regular folks are saving instead of spending. Even with mortgage rates at 3.5 percent, people are not buying homes. It begs the question what world are central bankers living in because all they talk about (if Janet Yellen can be taken at her word) is raising interest rates. On the one hand the public is being told the Central bank can control economic outcomes but can't control inflation – a concept that anyone can see is not only problematic but also ridiculous.

Why would they slow the economy down by raising interest rates when it is growing at a staggering and paltry pace already? This makes no sense in particular when the average citizen is confronting real economic hardship and despair and all the evidence (weak fundamentals) indicates this. If this is the path the US central banks takes, it will only prove what many already believe, that the central bank is for the wealth plutocratic class only and it only implements policy on their behalf that presents modern capitalism as merely socialism for the rich. If this is the case then maybe, just maybe, central banks shouldn't take on fiscal policy. In all honesty, maybe fiscal policy should be only implemented by folks the citizens vote on, or maybe we should vote for central bankers for that matter.

If I was given the authority first step I would take to destroy this Greenspan culture of hybrid fiscal/monetary policy would be to get rid of the Volcker rule in its entirety. Maybe this way we won't have to hear dumb azz Janet Yellen cite David Reifschneider anymore. Reifschneider for the record seems to be Yellen's go to guy. Whatever he says she holds on to like it was the word of God. Reifschneider is a Senior Economist for the Federal Reserve Bank and posits (really guesses without evidence) that bond purchases and low-rate promises should be enough for the Fed to deal with severe recession if such were to occur. This is why I think she has not been out into the real world for she is always saying the same thing, or rather something to the effect that US GDP growth to lift labor markets. Again, an observation I don't see even looking at BLS data, for there is no known value for potential economic output whether one is taking about labor or GDP – all of this is just speculative talk.

Simply put, central banks, in particular the US Federal Reserve should not be involved in developing, formulating or implementing fiscal policy. This should be left in the hands of the Treasury department in my opinion. One should ask what is their policy and where would we be if they couldn't buy assets? Since 2008, the US Federal Reserve bank has amassed $2.5 trillion in Treasury securities and $1.8 trillion of mortgage-backed securities (maybe even more) through its asset-purchase programs, yet we still have deplorable growth and horrific levels of unemployment if you read between the lines. What will be next? Will we follow the lead of Japan and start to buy exchange-traded funds (ETFs), or the ECB and begin to purchase corporate debt? Or even worse follow the path of Prime Minister Modi in India and remove cash from circulation? It is even easier to do in The US with electronic/digital money. More so given that today, money has no real value in and of itself due to separation of them from the original sources of money – gold and silver. Use to be a time when paper money just represented how much gold and silver we had, but not anymore. Add this to the massive depreciation and devaluation of money over past decades, a cashless society could be a real manifestation. But I regress.

All I am saying is that the philosophical acceptance of Greenspan economics has shown the ineffective, foolish and disconnection from reality that Fed policy is, and that we need to move beyond the make believe boundaries of Central bank policy (guessing) before it is too late. It is impossible to look at all economic activity in a contrived environment, under a contrived lens in which all stating points begin with full employment, inflation at 2 percent, and interest rates atnormal longer-run levels. Honestly, like the Euro, the Federal Reserve Bank was flawed from birth.

Trumpsessive Trumpulsive Disorder (TTD)

Some may be aware that in addition to Statistics, I also teach Neuroanatomy and Behavior. I have a keen fascination with brain physiology and functionality as it relates to behavior. True, I have interest biases such as the retinohypothalamic pathway, synaptic plasticity in the hippocampus and the hypothalamus-pituitary-adrenal axis (HPA) role in immunology. Likewise there are areas I have serious issues with and disdain for such as contrived abnormal behavior and mental illness as defined by any version of the DSMR. But with this said, I have decided to put aside this personal locution and consider the introduction of a new disorder that I will describe as Trumpsessive Trumpulsive Disorder (TTD).

As it is known, obsessions are irrational, disturbing thoughts that intrude into consciousness. Likewise, compulsions are repetitive actions performed to alleviate obsessions. These have become more prevalent in my opinion after the recent general election which saw Donald Trump win 83 percent of the geographical region of the United States and approximately 3,000 of the 3,143 counties in the US when compared to Hillary Clinton.

What is this abnormal behavior? For starters it is emblematic of symptomology of denial and irrational thoughts that are not grounded in fact or reality. Basic symptomology includes, incessant name calling of Trump and his supporters, violent and destructive outburst directed toward Trump and his supporters and even violence in the form of vandalism and the destruction of property. This can be detected on many of the social media platforms across the internet and even in the print and broadcast of mainstream media.

On the first level, it is evinced in the continuous description of Trump and his supporters as being described as 'dumb,' 'ignorant,' racist,' 'un or undereducated,' and 'bigoted' among others. Never mind that these portrayals are blanket stereotypes and generalizations applied to all equally whom supported Trump, regardless of race, ethnicity and educational attainment, the hilarity is that these same people would be offended for example if one were to generalize that all black men wearing hoodies were thugs or all blacks are lazy. They are the same cats that purport being tolerant to all and get their feelings in a bind when we talk of Muslims and immigrants in similar blanket terms. These are the same folk that state overtly a business owner cannot refuse a customer service based on race, ethnicity and sexual orientation, but you can if they support a different political view or voted for Trump. Thus this disorder is real since it demonstrates that these people say they want blacks, women, Latino, LGBTs and Hispanic all to have a seat at the table, unless they are republican, conservation and the cruncher – they voted for Trump.

Another tale-tale sign is social media activity. Typically all is either emotional vitriolic attacks against those whom support Trump or even RT a positive Trump story. Or maybe they always RT anything anti-Trump. This was all speculation until I tested it. How did I test it you query? My methodology was as follows: 10 I counted people whom retweet a minimum of 5 anti-Trump tweets (these met the criterion in the prior paragraph), 2 Respond to said tweet with all included to the tweet, 3 count the attacks and tag team attacks.

Example 1: The tweet in essence said the people voted for Hitler like they voted for Trump, #Heisnotmypresident. My response was that Hitler was appointed Chancellor of Germany by Paul von Hindenburg and assumed presidency upon death of Hindenburg – he was never voted on by the citizenry.

It appears fact is the worst enemy for the person suffering from TTD. My response drew vilification from several group tweets and eventually stopped for my follow up tweet was one in which I use frequently: Facts do not cease to exist because they are ignored– Aldous Huxley.

Example 2: This tweet asserted that the Carrier deal was just corporate welfare and thus no big deal. My response was that Obama was the king of corporate welfare – Boeing, Dell, Caterpillar, Chevron (even United Technologies) & gave us the Targeted Investment Program & the Temporary Liquidity Program not tomention TARP or the auto bailout. The results were the same as before, however instead of addressing the content, they resulted to repetitive actions performed to alleviate their obsessions (compulsion) in the form of calling me stupid and uneducated.

The severe or what I call TTD (i) are those with delusional symptomology. These ignore fact entirely and actually pretend that Trump is not their President. This is just like saying they think they are Jesus Christ or that the Easter bunny and Santa Klaus are real. These are also dangerous. They can destroy property, physically assault and attack Trump supporters and manifest delusion of grandeur that may be hazardous to themselves and all around them. These can be observed in threatening to kill Trump or his supporters or celebrating harm inflicted on a Trump supporter as we say in Chicago and regarding the Gatlinburg fires. But they are easily distracted about a story on Kanye West, a new Beyoncé video or celebrity awards show. It is even worse in mainstream media outlets.

Media outlets are mainly considered mainstream if they are from large cities on the east and west coast. Their level of TDD (i) is disturbing. They characteristically relinquish objectivity for partisan opinion making manipulated into being projected as news. They have even resorted to the use of Orwellian Newspeak proffered directly from the Oceana Ministry of Truth creating what they now call 'Fake News.' Fake News being anything they disagree with but more importantly, that does not metamorphasize from their pens, desk, computers or intellectual acumen. They even question the rules as most sore losers do after the fact. It seems end the Electoral College is retro chic currently. Even changing the senate and obviating the Connecticut Compromise so that rural voters cannot have the same or more power than urban voters because they know best and used to getting a trophy even when they do not earn one. Next it will be changing the rules of the World Series to where it is not the number of games won, but rather the total number of runs scored that determines the champion. This is simply delusional behavior.

TTD is real and it is just as much a sociopathy or psychopathy as gang banging and lynching. There isn't a psychopharmacological treatment for it yet nor hotline, albeit safe spaces can be found at your local university or DNC office.

When Democratic Arrogance
Becomes Whining Tantrums

Weeks after the Presidential election and it appears that some folks are still very much in their feelings. Each day it seems that no matter what the President elect says or does, it is problematic for this segment of the electorate and if given attention to, is considered to be some sort of dangerous attempt to "normalize' the behavior of a person they consider pathological and profoundly perilous.

This week it ranges from Trumps taking calls from the leaders of Pakistan, President of Kyrgyzstan Almazbek Atambayev or Taiwan, to his cabinet selections. However, any clinician worth their professionalism would note that these are just secondary to the main issue which is that as opposed to accepting reality they prefer to remain in a delusory state of denial, displacement and projection. This became clear to me after I heard the entire two hour and thirty-eight minute exchange between the Trump and Clinton campaign teams at Harvard this past week.

Obviously, there remains a significant level of grief for losing and animosity against Trump for winning the 2016 Presidential election. Thus no matter what the president elect does, will always be seen negatively. I saw this same sort of bitterness and angst displayed by the GOP and Clinton staffers when Obama won his 2008 run for the presidency.

Although Trump has thus far selected accomplished people who have made a mark in their chosen fields of expertise, many liberals are upset because he has not placed career politicians the likes of Clinton or Kerry in such slots as Obama did, although he ran on this as part of his platform. More indicative of this rage can be observed when they attempt to buttress their interpretations via argument, then seem unable to make any critical comment without invoking Hitler comparisons or worse, vilifying these selections as being images of racism or sexism, or the final election outcome being due to the influence of hackers and Russian meddling as a blogger I frequently read noted.

They ignore the fact that many in middle America outside of the urban landscape perceive that the Democrat party derides the concept of working hard, seem to care about not enforcing laws or supporting the men/women whom they frequently send off to fight in unnecessary wars and have more concern for illegal/undocumented aliens or foreign refugees than thepeople born here – especially the poor and homeless.

Accurate or not, they see the Federal government as a business and think it should be run like a business the way they run their households like businesses. These are some of the same people that gave Obama a chance although he had no business experience and what they see as the result is an America where race relations, poverty, employment opportunity and economic security has gotten worse. They considered Hillary Clinton fairly but concluded she was not in touch with their life experiences, and like Obama, had never in her life run anything on the level of a business. Not to forget that when President Elect Obama filled his cabinet with political elites, academics and Ivy League professors, there was no complaints. But with Trump bringing in competent people with success in the real world to be his advisors, it is evident that he desires folk that want to put the US before using their government positions to make money for themselves. These people already have money and such selections demonstrate that it is Trump's goal to run the government like a business.

Even when he follows through on a promise to keep that Indiana Carrier plant from moving to Mexico he is mocked. Yet there was no problem with Obama when he gave $500 million to Solyndra and even called Solyndra a success when he visited the company although most experts considered the company a failure. This is what most Americans see, and they consider these types of actions as arrogant responses of cry-baby sore losers. Not to mention we all know that he gave Solyndra this money as a favor to Rep. Pete Stark of California so he would push the ACA out of the House health committee.

Trump is putting together a business leadership coterie of advisers that understand the global economic market. This thus far has proven to be a group of folk that will not be prisoner to special interest. Which is another reason many are turned off by democrats whining and making excuses as if the general populous is so dumb that on our own examination, we are not supposed to see through the artificial veneer that you project Hilary Clinton to be. We, no matter what you tell us we should think or believe will never see Hillary as being smarter than us, let alone as successful as Trump, who although began with a large loan from his father, built his business with hard work and not with $250,000 a pop 45 minute speeches.

Democrats have to stop whining and confront the actuality that they are out of touch and have been out of touch and only have themselves to blame and no one else, so stop crying and pointing fingers at contrived bullshit ranging from James Comey, Fake news, or anything else. It is unfathomable as to how you could not see this coming. This was not an isolated event. Not only did HRC lose, but the Democratic Party also loss on the state level only holding a majority in 31 of the 98 legislative bodies across America.

Continuing to blame others for their own failures is a major indication that losing on this level for Democrats may only get worse in the coming years if they do not do some somber reflection and soul searching. And I say this because it appears they have learned nothing as evidenced by re-appointing 76 year old California Representative Nancy Pelosi as the Minority Leader of the House. In her own words she recently indicated how out of touch she and her party is when she stated: "I don't think people want a new direction. Our values unify us and our values are about supporting America's working families. That's one that everyone is in agreement on. What we want is a better connection of our message to working families in our country, and that clearly in the election showed that that message wasn't coming through."

Yes it looks bad for the democrats when they don't comprehend that speaking at or down to others and basically ordering them to do something that they singularly have decided as being unacceptable, and calling the names because they don't, isn't communicating, nor is it a message.

War of Taxes

Around 600 years ago in England there was a war. It was between the House of Lancaster and the House of York and was called ex post facto the Wars of the Roses. It was a petty and bloody war and ended when Richard III, the last Yorkist king, was defeated by Henry Tudor founder of the house of Tudor at the battle of Bosworth in 1485. We may be in for a similar metaphorical history making period of time if the tea leaves read from Brexit, the election of Donald Trump, and with Italian voters rejecting Prime Minister Matteo Renzi's referendum on constitutional reforms and the established world order with a "no" vote this past Sunday. If so, an ample title for this allegory could be the "War of Taxes."

Here in America, liberals have been so caught up on raising taxes on the wealthy that they missed the picture worldwide in terms on how these policies impact not only the world transnational economics but also the common citizen. This means that tax policy has to consider global and national economic interest equally.

As it stands, Ireland with a 12.5% corporate tax rate, has one of the lowest in the world. The federal corporate tax rate in the U.S. is thirty-five percent. Thus using basic math, if a company constructs a factory in Ireland that produces $1 million in profit, it will pay $125,000 in Irish tax compared to $350,000 that it would pay if it built the same factory in the U.S. This is a large difference seeing that the Organization for Economic Co-operation and Development (OECD) notes that the U.S. has the highest corporate income tax rate among its 35 industrialized member nations. What does this mean? Well knowing that Ireland is in the midst of a deep recession, the last thing there economic policy needs is to run-off foreign investment.

The U.K. has a similar economic problem. But after their June 23 Brexit vote to leave the European Union, under the leadership of U.K. Prime Minister Theresa May, they are going out of their way to comfort international companies to show that the U.K. will become an even better place to do business. Although what the U.K. corporate tax policy will be (whether she would be willing to embrace a suggested cut to 15% or to cut the rate by 2020 to 17%), the British government commitment to lower corporation tax is being well received and it is certain that in the future, it will be significantly lower than current levels and would give the nation the lowest corporate-tax rate among G-20 nations. Presently the U.K. corporate tax rate is 20%, which is one of the lowest in the G-20 and the same as Russia, Turkey and Saudi Arabia.

President elect Donald Trump has also expressed the importance of addressing the U.S.corporate tax rate. If we look beyond the G20 to the top 188 economic nations, the U.S.'s corporate tax rate is the third highest in the world, lower only than the United Arab Emirates' rate of 55 percent and Puerto Rico's rate of 39 percent, with the worldwide average corporate tax rate being 22.5 percent. Trump has proposed reducing the US federal tax from 35% to 15%. If this happens, in particular with a GOP dominated House and Senate, we may see the possibility of additional cuts in other nations. Steven Mnuchin, Trumps U.S.Treasury Secretary-nominee is already on record saying he wants to make tax reforms to increase job growth his main priority.

Before you say that Trump economic policy is impractical, be reminded that the U.S. is not the only country pushing for lower corporate tax rates. In 2015 Italy moved to lower its national corporate tax rate 24% starting in 2017 and Canada and Japan are just two of other countries currently in the process of lowering their corporate tax rates to attract new transnational businesses. Canada currently has a corporate income tax rate of 26.7 per cent. Even Japan, in an effort to promote growth just reduced its corporate tax rate to 30%. Germany along with Ireland made big cuts in an effort to attract corporate investment more than a decade ago and it has proffered effective.

All of the above may be a forewarning of what may be on the horizon – a war of corporate tax rates around the globe. This should only be expected since after losing regulatory requirements and closing tax loopholes, the only thing left to promote domestic economic growth in pragmatic terms is to reduce ones national corporate tax rate. Moreover, given that the U.S. doesn't have a value-added tax (VAT or federal sales tax), having higher corporate tax rates will continue to serve as an impediment to economic growth domestically in terms of increased wages and jobs. It is not a requirement that we turn into a Greece before we learn the lessons of Greece. So although the War of the Roses is history, maybe 600 years from now, history books will be talking about the war of taxes.

TV Watchers Miss the Taiwan & Pakistan Big Picture

There were several kerfuffle's that the alphabet networks and their mindless audience pushed as being calamitous actions taken by Donald Trump this past week. The two that caught my attention occurred while listening to NPR and applied to Taiwan and Pakistan. Seems that Mr. Trump accepting calls from the democratically elected Taiwanese President Tsai Ing-wen and responding to a similar call from Pakistani Prime Minister Nawaz Sharif were appalling, shocking and destabilizing, averring that the President Elect supposedly upended the traditional convention on how to deal with Chinese geopolitics, consequently destroying nearly 40 years of standard US diplomacy regarding Taiwan, and our relations with India via Pakistan.

This response was predictable based on how the MSM media has dealt with Trump and hung on his each and every word and tweet. Those critical of Trump say that his actions are just thoughtless blundering mistakes and signs of his ineptness in foreign policy. This was not the case. These single-minded individual elite's infer that this is a reflection of Trump being a political novice. I take the contrarian view and assert it is the complete opposite.

The US relationship with China has continuously been all over the place since the end of the Nixon Administration. Likewise, we can only thank Obama with his droning and unauthorized raids in Pakistan (Bin Laden included) as only bring about more political destabilization with respect to diplomatic actions with the nation. It is as if the pundits do not see how their speculations on behalf of ratings and sensationalization, are being overstated.

Let's start with Taiwan and China. After the Ford administration, upon taking office, President Jimmy Carter was in such a big hurry to normalize relations with China that in 1978 Congress got involved to make sure that America's mutual defense treaty with Taiwan would not fall by the wayside. So under the leadership of Massachusetts Senator Ted Kennedy, a bipartisan congressional alliance proposed the Taiwan Relations Act after Carter ignored their concerns. In essence congress indicated that the United States would not hesitate to aid Taiwan if it was invaded by China going against terms of diplomacy established in 1949. Carter like today's media pundits were afraid this would upset and hurt China's feelings.

By the Time Bill Clinton was in office, a 'One China' policy and de-recognition of Taiwan was in full effect and since his Administration; we have not been honest in our foreign policy objectives. So in simple terms, the current reaction to Trump's actions in regards to China-Taiwan may be unhelpful and may hurt the fledgling Taiwan democracy and should be considered more important than papers and air time advertisement media outlets sell.

All we can take away from this is that Trump is making good on his tough talk on China and that he will shake the ways of old off and not be restrained by the bureaucratic practices of the old political establishment guard. Just by going against 37 years of China-US diplomatic protocol of the "one China" policy the US accepts and respects without query. No US President or President-elect has ever called a Taiwanese leader in recent decades. Trump's independence is what the story should be about not to mention two things are abrogated from the popular analysis: (1) Chiang Kai-shek is no longer the leader of Taiwan and (2) Trump isn't the first president or president-elect since 1979 to have communicated directly with a president of Taiwan noting that if memory serves me correctly Reagan did the same thing when he was president elect.

Fact is politicians on both sides of the isle have been reconsidering albeit very quietly the US-China-Taiwan relationship since 1989 (Tiananmen Square) and the question if they really want Taiwan to unify with China. In fact I bet I could find support if I really wanted to be super-duper accurate that since Tiananmen Square, the US have been selling more and more weapons to Taiwan, but this is mere speculation on my part. The point is Trump has not only shown himself thus far to be an effective negotiator, he has also been continuously underestimated every step of the way so far by folk whom think they know it all in the media and has proven that there is more than one way to skin a cat metaphorically.

Adding Pakistan to the mix, we see the same thing if we are truly objective before we are outraged. It is clear that President-elect Donald Trump may be amenable to similar eccentric methods regarding bilateral ties with the nation and Pakistani Prime Minister. In this case, the media analysts have called Trump's actions on one end ridiculous and the other distressing. Based on what I read all he said was that he thought Sharif was "a terrific guy" and wanted to visit what he described as a fantastic country with great people speaking of Pakistan. What all of this suggest is that Trump is not the traditional status quo political cat to the disdain of the traditional American political elite and mainstream media. All he wants is for the US to be a part in trying to secure peace between India and Pakistan. What's wrong with that?

The problem is that the reaction of the US media may be the biggest issue with respect to both China and Taiwan, and Pakistan and India by blowing all of this out of proportion in their desire to "get Trump" by any means necessary. Fact is that US foreign policy is fluid and changes and over stating events as the aforementioned can do more harm than good. It is as if Trump taking a phone call is more problematic for the Chinese than Obama selling four missile carrying frigates and billions in other weaponry to Taiwan. Then there is the fact that Trump isn't even in office yet and has not even laid out any foreign policy. So just calm down and wait for something tangible to report on and not personal bias in the form of made-up fears.

The Forgotten South of Sudan

As we continuously hear from the Obama Administration about Aleppo, among the other international events laid at the feet of President Obama's foreign policy we do not hear of inclusive of Yemen is South Sudan. Established after a referendum vote to secede from the northern part of Sudan and the Khartoum government, and once touted as a way to formalize peace to Sudan's long-running civil war, this small oil rich nation has dissolved into pure blood stained disorder. Even famous actors the likes of George Clooney and Don Cheadle advocated for its existence as being a humanitarian necessity to show the people we in the west cared.

For years prior to its formulation (not formation), the US supported rebels in the south of Sudan. After the nation of South Sudan was formed, the U.S. continued to provide billions of dollars in military and security assistance to the fledgling country under the Obama Administration and Hillary Clinton's State Department. In 2011 then Secretary of State Clinton, at a major conference on South Sudan in 2011, spoke of her visions for the future of South Sudan. Ironically, in the same year in which President Obama employed a technicality to get a Child Soldiers Prevention Act (CSPA) exemption for South Sudan.

The logic was feculent and two fold. First being that the law could not be applied to a newly formed nation that recently became independent and second, the administration wanted the country to get on firm ground before the US made any statutory request of its military. Meaning that since the countries subjected to CSPA were already in existence, they could not add the South Sudan to thelist. The Obama administration also openly advocated their support for the Sudan People's Liberation Army (SPLA). The SPLA according to human rights group worldwide have been documented to have engaged in numerous human rights violations, including but not limited to rape and extrajudicial killings (nice UN saying for murder).

However since the celebration of South Sudan as the world's newest member state in 2011, a political rivalry between the Dinka President Salva Kiir and the then Nuer Vice President Riek Machar erruptrd dissolving the nation into a civil war along ethnic lines. Since then more than 1 million South Sudanese have fled to neighboring countries like Uganda and many thousands more have been slaughtered, tortured or raped. One UN report noted that South Sudanese army soldiers had raped thousands of women and girls as a reward for their service instead of being paid salaries. Others had been used as part of ritual cannibalistic activities or burned alive.

But none of this mattered to the Obama Administration. Although in his formal recognition statement for the Republic of South Sudan as a sovereign and independent state he described it as a "historic achievement" after "the darkness of war," his policy has proven the opposite and has resulted in more bloodshed and insecurity by not ending the use of child soldiers on the one hand and by turning a blind eye to the atrocities committed by the nation he pushed to establish on the other. What the president once hailed as one of his foreign policy success stories, is now merely a failed state in reality - unless it is the desire for Nobel Peace prize winning presidents to leave nations in the ruinous aftermath of war (Yemen, Libya and Syria also included).

Obama in concert with his National Security Advisor Susan Rice vehemently led the crusade for the creation of South Sudan, but since then, we have only seen daily tribal hostilities continuing to fester. Add to this that the economic condition is following a similar descending path and that state sponsored repression remains a major impediment to any form of democratic government, what we get from the President is silence or troops. Nor does he address how the ongoing violence rests as a massive obstacle to peace which on its own serves as a catalyst for the continuing genocide in Darfur and a growing militarization of the party's involved. In particular since the present administration continues to honor the authorization of more than $120 million in U.S. military assistance and over $20 million in arms sales since FY2013 and an addition request for $30 million in military assistance for South Sudan for FY2017.

Now it would be insincere to place all of this at the feet of President Obama since a sizable amount of his foreign policy was advocated for and proposed by Hillary Clinton. As a presidential candidate, Clinton consistently presented her foreign policy experience as a major justification for her being president, although she never spoke openly about her desire to intervene in Libya or her role in the failed Russian "reset." More importantly, there was no mention of the outcome of her efforts in South Sudan. True in 2012 she openly stated her disparagement of the use and recruitment of children as soldiers, however it was a position in dire contrast to her part in allowing South Sudan to receive US military support via her approval of waivers to the nation while it used children as fighters. Still Clinton's handling of South Sudan and how the new nation descended into a calamitous civil war that involved the use of thousands of child soldiers is rarely reported.

When President Obama leaves the White House next January, people worldwide will question his foreign policy. This will likely be partisan but the objective individual will note from Yemen to Libya and Syria to South Sudan – he was afailure. Moreover, he managed to make social and economic situations in these places worse. But in Sudan he will be remembered for creating a state and leaving it to rot; a place where he waived to the prohibition on the use of child soldiers in an untried country that is acknowledged as being one of the most corrupt in the world and the home of a 4-year-old civil war where US installed leaders have used their positions to rob the country of its wealth, while at the same time creating one of the greatest humanitarian disasters today – in essence an embarrassment for the Obama administration. As a newly formed country, the future looked bright for South Sudan and its vast oil reserves. But realty has shown us otherwise, that effective foreign policy demands more than words and dumping huge sums of money in the hands of installed puppets.

A Clash of Cultures: Trump versus the Media Elite

The Election of Donald Trump resulted in very severe out-break of what I call Trumpsessive Trumpulsive Disorder (TDD). It is something that in my opinion has been created by a uniquely disingenuous cult of protagonist I simply call elitist east coast media. This is not a geographical description but rather a cultural ethos that can also be applied to big city media cats in general.

From the very beginning there was a bias in the Clinton versus Trump narrative and even before then, the Clinton versus Sanders narrative as presented by this media cult. If we take the example of race, nonstop coverage has hurled the same invectives towards Trump including but not limited to bigot, racist and xenophobic. They ignored any mention of Clinton regarding her categorization of blacks as super predators or how she loaded her campaign coffers with big money from the corporate prison industrial complex. They never reviewed any of her past including her 2008 attempt to receive the democratic nomination for president including how her campaign floated around an image of Barack Obama in African/Muslim attire. The media especially the New York Times or Washington Post never discussed this instead they continuously attacked Trump as being a racist who was anti-black, anti-Mexican, anti-immigrant and anti-Muslim who repeatedly made insensitive comments about the afore-mentioned groups. With regards to Sanders several DNC top officials including Debbie Wasserman-Schultz were forced to resign after WikiLeaks emails revealed that not only were they favoring HRC, they were also trying to present Bernie Sanders as an atheist albeit he was a Jew because it was easi-er to get people to vote against an atheist. Instead of address-ing this, they floated fake news that this was a Russian plot and continued to attempt to program the citizenry that Clin-ton was winning and would win by a wide margin. Wik-iLeaks also revealed the high level extent to which collusion between the DNC, Clinton and the East coast media elites was occurring.

What the Trump coverage revealed is that these me-dia big shots considered Trump as being alien to them, as not being one of them and even precluded this same judgment down upon his supporters. It is as if these elite east coast me-dia folk are mad at the folk whom voted for Trump, as if they are the gatekeepers saying we voted the wrong way, or how dare you by pass our suggestions of how bad Mr. Trump is and make up your minds for yourself without our blessings – how dare you go against us who are smarter and know better for you. But are they?

Now to be objective, maybe they are. Slate, Salon, the Washington Post and NY Times practically served as a PR firms for camp HRC. From NBC's Chuck Todd hosting dinner for Jennifer Palmieri and John Podesta to John Podes-ta hosting a dinner for all of the media fat cats at his house, they do have an insight into the HRC camp that the average person doesn't have. This is what I call the modern equiva-lent of the god ole boy's network.

The website 538 along with Slate, Salon, the Washington Post, CNN, the Nation and NY Times along with many others told us Trump would never become the Republican nominee, let alone President. They told us that all of these states were in play like Arizona, Ohio, Texas and Georgia when they were not. Although it would be easier for them to say "hey, we fucked up, we were wrong," they will likely spend the next 8 years (if Trump gets two terms) trying to prove the electorate that they were wrong, not them.

The media doesn't know how to cover Trump but hasn't the balls to admit this. They condemn Trump for turning politics into reality TV theater but they have been presenting politics as theater for the last two decades. For example, they criticize Trump for his use of Twitter but they use Twitter in the same manner and even more than the President-elect. It is the ultimate hypocrisy reveal for political journalist the likes of Joy Ann Reid, Jamelle Bouie, Marc Lamont Hill, Jake Tapper, Jamil Smith, Rachel Maddow, Paul Krugman, or a Don Lemmon, when they do the same thing in an effort to maximize their outreach and popularity. Would it be so hard for them just to admit they just hate the fact he uses twitter to by pass them?

Since his election the MSM has changed or altered little in their coverage of President Elect Donald Trump. It is a period of media coverage that is no doubt unique. The clear outcome is that the elite east coast mainstream big city media holds Donald Trump to one standard and democrats, in particular President Obama and HRC to another. They have even invented a new excuse to cover for their lack of ethics and intellect – Fake news. Fake news propaganda is a cover up to justify the failures of the political media's coverage of the election. In addition it is an overt attempt to marginalize voices and views outside of their belief orientation and personal collective reality yet in basic terms a new age conspiracy theory. By doing such, it allows them to ignore real news stories and dwell on impractical and unsubstantiated figments of their make believe world. For example, they ignore or are weeks late on covering the #NDPL and the Standing Rock Sioux in the Dakota's. Why, because Obama a Democrat was President. You can't mention that while a black liberal progressive democrat is serving as president that under his administration water cannons are being employed on women and children in sub-freezing temperatures at close range, that law enforcement and federal officers are shooting people with rubber bullets and attack dogs are being let loose on native Americans because it would not be a god look. But you can best believe that if Trump was president they would have plastered it all over the 24 hour news cycle opining that this is a representation of Trump's racist, sexist and white supremacy views. This is why the fake Russia news story is important. If they didn't have this, maybe they would have to cover that there were more votes than voters in more than one-third of Detroit precincts.

This is fake news by omission and own its own it is comical. Just think, the same cats that gave us falsified Iraq news coverage in 2003, said that only a score of folk were killed during the invasion of Panama, cry about Aleppo but never what is happening in Yemen or Mosul, have the audacity to complain about the conspiracy theory of fake news as being why they were wrong regarding this past presidential election. Or worse that Russia cost HRC the election, as if they told HRC not to campaign in Michigan or Wisconsin or not to appear in Lousisana during the massive flooding. The political media doesn't understand their job. It is to cover the news, to be journalist, not create the news and predict election outcomes. Fake news is the new conspiracy theory, and it is being promulgated by the biggest culprit of the production of fake news – the elite east coast mainstream media.

The Alt-Left is Real & It's Run By White City Cats

I had never heard of the Alt-Right until Hillary Clinton introduced the term in our lexicon during a speech she gave in Reno this past August. Now I had heard of the alternative right, which had nothing to do with media, but rather an ideology that was juxtapose to the mainstream GOP. Now maybe you had read or heard about it but not me, in particular in the manner in which she framed it as being a platform for white supremacy, which is far from the truth. And like the sheep in the heard, most, especially liberal democrats engaged in Orwellian newspeak to make it real and tangible. However, if the Alt-Right is as dastardly as folk make it out to be, the Alt-Left is even more destructive and fascist. Yes, the Alt-Left is real and it is run mostly by white city cats. What is the Alt-Left? Well it is the diametric opposite of the Alt-Right and is manifested in action and word through extreme intolerance.

The examples of Alt-Left activities are both sickening and too numerous to name and I say this because I know if their actions were directed toward President Barack Obama for instance, these activities would be seen in a different vein. Let us look at voter intimidation. The left has always advocated that voter intimidation is horrible and intolerant. There are even laws on the books that note that such is a criminal act. But when it is directed towards electors of the Electoral College, there is not a single statement of outrage from democrats or the mainstream media opined against these occurrences. When people are receiving death threats urging them to change their vote to support Hillary Clinton it seem as it is swept under the rug. These threats are not coming from the Alt-Right, but rather the Alt-Left. Or when the daughter of the President Elect is verbally accosted while riding on an airplane with her kids by two gay men, there is no outrage and it is presented as being acceptable comportment. Now mind you if this was done to the wife of President Obama, I can only imagine the outrage. Even if it were just a women in general with her kids, no one in their civil mind would consider this as being acceptable behavior.

I used to the think the left was anti-bullying but clearly they are not. This in simple terms in bullying. I take it is okay to bully people who do not think like you or maintain the same political beliefs as one does. But outside of this it is wrong. Or the young college student at Bryn Mawr College who was harassed and sent death threats for supporting Donald Trump and now has been forced to leave school for her safety. Or the University of Pittsburg student who set up a Trump table at his university. This is the Alt-Left although they are constantly speaking on ending hate and violence,these remain their go to weapons of choice. These students didn't ask for or need a safe space, they were amenable to open dialogue and discussion and put their views out for all to acknowledge. Nicholas Kristof said it best: We progressives believe in diversity and we want women, blacks, Latinos and Muslims at the table – er, so long as they aren't conservatives…We are fine with people who don't look like us as long as they think like us."

This is the closed-minded intolerant hypocrisy that defines the Alt-Left. How can the left incessantly speak about the necessity of tolerance and openness but write off the political beliefs of others they do not listen to or engage in dialogue with? Most of these representatives of the Alt-Left are educated urban white folk and maintain a descent capability of subject-verb agreement but they would rather vandalize, curse, yell and call others out of their name. I read that some do not want to do business with Trump supporters. Now if a baker or restaurant said the same about an Obama supporter or a gay couple, it would fall under the banner of bigotry and intolerance – I do not want to serve you because of your beliefs.

I suspected this rise of the Alt-Left would be problematic since their anti-trumps protest in Chicago, California and Portland. After Trump won, it became even more idiotic: a black man painting racist images on a black church in Mississippi, artist demanding Ivanka Trump take down paintings of their she bought down from her walls (thus the use of the term idiotic), a Muslim women in New York faking an attack by white Trump supporters while in the subway and singers refusing to perform at the inauguration while they have no problem performing for millions for known despots and murderous authoritarian dictators.

These safe space trophy babies are the embodiment of fascist ideology – my way or the highway, authoritarian cultural Marxist. Yes the Alt-Left is real and these cats are the fascist of tomorrow.

The Aleppo Misdirection

The mess in Syria has been going on for the past six years. There still is no clarity on the events there with the exception of the facts and the main fact that the US Nobel prize winning president is true to the play book of his predecessor George H.W. Bush. I wanted to write in detail about this a while ago but it was difficult to extract my attention from the humor of liberals whining because their loss to Trump and the sore loseritus was a gift I could not avoid writing about. But since the U.K., France and U.S. convened this special meeting of the UN Security Council, I had to go in, and I will explain.

I think since Obama announced months ago his plan to attack Mosul (as if he was telegraphing' to the terrorist, I mean moderates he supports in Iraq and Syria to get ready), he had not perceived that there was even the possibility that Aleppo would be liberated. Given this major lapse in judgement and reasoning, coalition forces have been back peddling ever since. It seems that the manipulation of language (Newspeak) was the first sign that things were all over the place regarding a standard approach on how to deal with Syria. I say Syria because Aleppo is really a misnomer. They say they just want to help and offer humanitarian aid for the more than a million residents of Aleppo although there is no equal concern for the civilians in Mosul or cities in Yemen. So to try and support their position that Assad must go, the Obama Administration created the term "Moderate Syrian Rebels."

To be truthful, there is no such thing as a moderate terrorist no more as there is a such thing as a moderate Crip or Blood, in particular with the fluid nature of all of the groups, the alliances they form and assorted reasons for fighting including but not limited to [1] forming a Sunni state run under Sharia law, [2] those who are fighting for autonomous rule (Kurds), and/or [3] the few that want to violently over throw the democratically elected Assad who won a sizable majority last election with more than 70% voter turnout. What has been documented is that militants who are integrated with terror groups like Jaysh al Fatah, Jabhat al Nusra, Ahrar al Sham and Nour al din al Zenki - all of them affiliated with the Al Qaeda terrorist network – are what Western coalition governments consider to be portions of the Free Syrian Army (FSA) and at the same time claim to be at war with.

Now before I dive into these so-called moderate rebels, I have to go back to the earlier supposition regarding Mosul and the Obama Administration. In all fairness, the operation to retake Mosul was not about destroying ISIS but rather to push ISIS back into Syria so they could focus all of their efforts on taking down Assad. Why do I say this? Well if one reads Carl von Clausewitz, typically the military objective is to close all escape routes and incessantly enclose the enemy and crush them. The Obama administration had planned operations from all sides with the exception of routes towards the Iraq-Syria border. Thus the objects would have to be removing these terrorist from Iraq and into Syria resulting in the PR circus of claiming a speedy victory in Mosul. But after three months this is not the case.

Mosul and Raqqa are the two major cities in the self-proclaimed IS caliphate. To destroy IS these must be destroyed. However, when Russia and Iran got involved, the Obama Administration never calculated that they would be able to sway so much influence with the present Iraqi government and subsequently were able to modify the U.S. battle plan to one that would encircle and attempt to destroy all ISIS/Al Qaeda affiliates in Mosul. This threw a wrench in the Administration's goal to engender a "Salafist principality" designed to break up or "Balkanize" Syria. It was the same play book used in Libya with the exception of a no-fly zone. So without a no-fly zone, the coalition had to result to other means – namely trying to protect the Salafist in Aleppo they had been funding and arming since they began this proxy war. This is why reports from Aleppo by the West are all over the place.

The information, if any we are getting from Aleppo is really no different than a Hollywood screen play. First the Obama Administration threatened the Russians saying that their planes would be shot down and their troops would be coming home in body bags while at the same time shipping tons of anti-aircraft weaponry to rebels in and around Aleppo when the Obama Administration were supposedly trying to achieve a cease fire. This was at the same time John Kerry was saying he was going to suspend discussions with the Russians regarding Syria, just after US ambassador to the UN, Samantha Power, vilified the Russian's for convening a special security council meaning to discuss coalition air-strikes that targeted Syrian government forces, killing more than 80 soldiers. The same US ambassador to the UN would weeks later confront the Russians again, using unverified reports accusing them in concert with Assad of murdering innocent civilians. Now all of this is hard for me to keep track of so I'm guessing it is the same for a lot of people. The reason why is because there never was or has been a civil war in Syria.

The Syrian revolution is a myth. Western Aleppo is being targeted because they resisted these U.S backed Salafist foreign terrorist and the record indicates that clearly more than a half a million civilians left the eastern portion of the city for the west for the same reason. The majority left in Eastern Aleppo are being held hostage by the terrorist or are terrorist and their families. Thus the remaining civilians in this area are being used as human shields and the query remains, if the US narrative of Assad murdering and bombing his own people is accurate, then why would they flee Eastern Aleppo and go to the part held by Assad forces? Makes no sense. Seven million have fled to government held sections over the past four plus years. But the media call these folk Assad supporters when in fact they may or may not be - they just don't support terrorist or believe that killing and destroying Syria is the best approach for improving their government.

We never check with organizations on the ground like the Aleppo Medical Association about the number of physicians working there because if we did we would see that there are more than 4000 working there and many are being paid by the Assad government (opposite of the narrative of western media). Unfortunately the rebels or opposition which are really terrorist prevent them from coming in and even giving their services. Add to this that Eastern Aleppo is under the control by the Al Nusura front (Al Qaeda in Syria), yet the Obama administration wants to protect these folk. The Free Idlib army are terrorist too. So given the US media isn't even on the ground in Aleppo, how can they verify their information? Verification isn't required when it is all for show bearing in mind the main goal has been and remains regime change in Syria. Just like in Iraq the goal is to create a shadow state in Syria to be controlled by and for the benefit of the West.

The more logical and truthful depiction is that Syrian civilians are at last able to flee from terror gangs that have held them under siege. But this is in contradiction to the reporting by Western media on Syria and Aleppo especially since the US and Western narrative about what has been going on in Aleppo and Syria, Assad and Syrian civilians is far removed from the facts. One has to wonder why they are never in Aleppo or even Syria, if so they are there rarely or else they would have been able to at least interview any one of the tens of thousands of civilians who have left areas once controlled by the motley collection terrorist groups. They preclude they hate the Assad government but never ask them if they do or fail to query as to how life was living under these terrorist groups – journalism 101. We see US ambassador to the UN Samantha Power refer to unverified reports of civilians being executed in Aleppo while asking at the same time if Syria, Iran or Russia have any shame. But they never seem to compare the devastation US coalition forces are delivering in Yemen or Mosul.

The actuality is Aleppo was invaded by Western-backed mercenary terrorist proxies, or fake moderate rebels, whom the Western governments have sponsored in an attempt to overthrow the government of Syria since July 2012. These same Western-backed mercenary terrorist proxies, or fake moderate rebels have turned the eastern side of the city into terror haven for a caliphate of manic Wahhabi jihadists that take more pleasure in chopping off heads than secular democratic rule. From Jeish al-Fatah (Army of Conquest) to Jabha Fatah al-Sham (Front for the Conquest of the Levant) and Fatah Halab (Conquest of Aleppo) they are all terrorist the U.S. supports and arms and would never engage in a ceasefire being implemented of any kind and the Obama administration knows this.

They understand that these groups must keep fighting if the breakup of Syria and the take-down of Assad is ever to be achieved. Otherwise, the Syrian national bank will remain free of western influence and will never be brought under the Bank of International Settlements and thus continue to operate without loans from the IMF which means they can decide their own foreign policy and that dream of a natural gas pipeline from Qatar to Turkey will never come to fruition. Moreover, Syria will not be made to submit to using GMO seeds. Recall one of the first things US did after the conquering of Iraq was to outlaw seeds stores and force Iraqi farmers to buy international GMO seeds (see order 81 Iraq).

Regardless of what comes out of Washington from the Administration or the media, Syria as Libya before it will be remembered as just another war crime committed by President Obama in the name of humanitarian intervention by the West when the real geopolitical aim was regime change for the fact remains that US or western security interests were never involved or at risk. Just as with Gaddafi, who never really ever threaten to massacre civilians, the same is true for Assad. Gaddafi, just as Assad currently, only went after rebels and similarly, offered them amnesty and free passage out if they would drop their weapons. In both cases, the "responsibility to protect", is just a fancy way to say it is okay to violate the sovereignty of another nation state.

As the Obama era comes to a close, what can be noted is that he will be remembered as the man who destroyed Libya (at the time Africa's most thriving nation) and will have nothing to show for his foreign policy in Syria with the exception of more than a half a million deaths and a Europe in consternation due to a colossal refugee and migrant crisis.

So expect for the amplification of anti-Syrian and anti-Russian newspeak in the US mainstream media to continue because the Syrian Army are continuously advancing through Aleppo and routing the US funded terrorist.

Obama's Sherman Moment

Just one day after President Barack Obama moved to expel thirty-five Russian expatriates, Russian President Vladimir Putin took the high road and turned the other cheek – an action that the Obama Administration surely did not anticipate and likely considered equally embarrassing. I suspect as others have also noted, that this was an attempt on Obama's behalf to close down the warming of relations with Russia that the incoming President Elect has signaled he was willing to attempt. Yes, this was indeed the ultimate F### you to the outgoing President. I am sure they will try to spin this in a positive. Maybe they will say Putin was wrong so he had no reason to capitulate in response, that there is no way he can retaliate (both of which are false) or make up new evidence of Russian hacking the U.S. to gather more anti-Russian sentiment.

Anyone with common sense can conclude that this isn't about Russia or even the election, but rather Obama and the failed policy purported by the Democratic left in America. As a lame duck, President Obama has placed the interest of the failing Democratic Party over the national security interest of the American people. His aversion for Donald Trump has led him to project and use the historical trained fear produced in the American people for decades to hate Russia – like the name of one of my favorite musical groups, a Cheap Trick. In a few months the Democratic Party and mainstream East coast media has turned liberal progressives into neocon war hawks.

Hilarity right? This re-invigorated blame-Russia ruse seemed to start a few years ago when Putin got hip to Obama's game after the February 2014 coup to overthrow the democratically elected President of Ukraine, Viktor Yanukovych. For some reason or another, the cat folk though was smart as sh## (Obama) didn't seem to recall that this was not the Yeltsin era, or that since then, Putin has managed to beat Obama to the punch in all of his foreign policy efforts like a chess grand master playing a beginner.

It was a foreign policy coup. Especially when you add to the calculus the just negotiated Turkey-Russia cease-fire agreement in Syria which can be stated is a consequence of Putin's leadership and involvement in the nation over the past year (an act that has successfully neutered American neo-liberal policy goals in their call for Assad to leave office). This is amazing seeing all of this has occurred after Erdogan's government shot down a Russian jet and years after Obama telling Medvedev on an open mic in 2012 that he would work more openly with Russia as a partner rather than a nemesis. Add to this Russia's improved relationship with Turkey, questions now come to the forefront regarding NATO's second largest Army coming under a significant level of influence under Putin and concerns about deteriorating relations between Turkey and the U.S. One could go further and even include this past December when Defense Secretary Ashton Carter, while in Bahrain stating that the U.S. had reached an agreement for Qatar to purchase a 5,000-kilometer early-warning radar to enhance its missile defenses (you can see a lot of Russia with this).

It is strange that Obama is doing all of this as he prepares to leave the Whitehouse. The Obama administration on the surface seems to be trying to provoke a direct confrontation with Putin while at the same time create a new cold-war foreign policy crisis for President-elect Donald Trump to deal with the minute he assumes the office of presidency.

Among other things, he has also stepped up arming and funding jihadist in Syria and has ratchetted up tensions with Putin not only in Syria, but also on his boarders by installing anti-ballistic missiles in Romania, Poland, and other nations (supposedly to protect Europe against Iranian missiles). Now to top it off, he has contrived fake Russian hacking. One sad consequence is that the Obama Administrations failure to find any solution to what is happening in Syria, diplomatic or otherwise, and how to defeat the Islamic State has resulted in historic U.S. allies in the region scratching their heads in confusion. Namely what is the position of the U.S.? What leverage if any do they have in the region and will they protect their interests in the region and how?

Even with these actions, the report the administration released detailing how the alleged hack occurred was not detailed at all. There was no mention of the fact that John Podesta was his own worse cyber enemy. It doesn't really fall into the category of hacking when you email your passwords around, lose a cell phone or respond to a password phishing email even a 6th graders known not to open. From what I read, most of the "detailed" report produced by the FBI/DHS talked about how cats can protect themselves from malware but little if anything about proving that the Russians were the source of the DNC or Podesta email leaks. Really it was replete of circumstantial evidence and oblique hints (innuendo).

Although the President promised to consult and work with Congress on this issue, he has not nor did he present them with a detailed report PROVIDING PROOF that the Russians did it or that the motive was to elect Donald Trump. It is easy to say that a car jacker stole your car for money, but to say why he needed the money and what the money would have been used for is another matter. Thus to state unequivocally that this Russian cyber hacking attempt was aimed at the U.S. presidential election to elect Trump by talking about hacking infrastructure in an effort to help prevent more hacking in the future does not suffice as PROOF.

Jerry Gamblin said "the Grizzly Steppe data it is disjointed, ambiguous and really doesn't provide any actionable data for most companies." Cybersecurity expert Jeffrey Carr wrote: "It merely listed every threat group ever reported on by a commercialcybersecurity company that is suspected of being Russian-made and lumped them under the heading of Russian Intelligence Services (RIS) without providing any supporting evidence that such a connection exists." Errata Security CEO RobGraham pointed out that, one of the signatures detects the presence of "PAS TOOL WEB KIT," a tool that's widely used by literally hundreds, and possibly thousands, of hackers in Russia and Ukraine, most of whom are otherwise unaffiliated and have no connection to the Russian government. Lastly to quote Robert M. Lee, CEO and Founder of the critical infrastructure cyber security company Dragos stated "There is no mention of the focus of attribution in any of the White House's statements." In simple terms, the white house is guessing and giving an opinion that can't even point directly to the Russian government.

Some have suggested (which I agree with) that Obama is trying to embarrass Trump and that he is trying to provoke the President elect into a cyber war with Russia (which I disagree with). However, Putin's response demonstrates that Obama's new sanctions and expulsions is a reflection of his weakness in foreign policy. This sentiment was echoed in the comments made by Russian foreign ministry spokeswoman Maria Zakharova when she said, "Obama and his illiterate foreign policy team" was just a bunch of "losers, angry and shallow-brained."

Democrats are now in unfamiliar water – taking the same policy positions regarding Russia as their alter-ego Republicans. This is comical by itself, complaining about authoritarian executive leadership abroad when they sponsor and support similar leadership in Saudi Arabia and Bahrain. Plus there is the added discord at home post-election which demonstrated how the Democrats incessant use and presentation of identity politics obviated the largest voting bloc in America from its constituency - working-class whites. Yes Obama can see the writing on the wall and has decided to resort to past lessons of history using the example of General William Tecumseh Sherman scorched earth/slash and burn approach. Yep, Obama trying to hem in Trump, and burn all of America in the process just to throw shade.

The Elephant Grass of the Democratic Party

The hissy fits of the Democratic Party over the election victory of Donald Trump continue. If one pays strict attention to their whining, it all seems to be a cloak for inherent and clandestine fears based on emotion more so than pragmatism and reason. It reminds me of how one of my uncle friends described being in Vietnam when I was between 11 and 12 years old (1973-74). He told me about how what he would never forget the sounds of war, were the marshy fields he and his company would be dropped off in, feet tall above the head of Elephant grass. He said these fields were packed with booby traps but what scared him most was not being able to see around him. The tall grass in addition to the grown-man high ant mounds, concealed the unexpected, seeing that the Elephant grass was tall enough to hide an entire military detail ready for ambush.

I suspect that this is how the democrats feel. As if they were dropped off in a field of Elephant grass, not know what the future holds in store for them. Could it be they expect to be invalidated by Trump and the GOP? Could it be that they fear Trump will make good on his campaign promises and lead to the destruction of the Democratic Party for years to come? Or could it be it will show the US citizenry how democratic policy has placed America in its current predicament?

All are possibilities. Let's face it, no matter how democrats and the media try to paint Obama's eight years as a success, math shows the opposite. The math, as pure science reveals the truth that politically the democrats are powerless and stuck in a destitute defensive posture. Thus their primary weapon is crying and/or attacking the incoming administration through mere emotional displacement. Jamil Smith attacks Trump on his "intellectual laziness" suggesting that this "may be the most dangerous thing about him," and that "Vladimir Putin wanted Donald Trump to be presidentof the United States, and the Russian government deliberately tried to help him win the election." Jamile Bouie suggest that "Trump is defined by his shameless disregard, and even disdain, for the bonds that hold political life together." Or in the case of some, they simply stick to praise of Putin as being evidence of incompetence and dishonesty. All unfounded and groundless allegations pure in rhetoric singularly.

All of these are just emotional invective. These writers will never back up their words with tangible accomplishments of President Obama to compare these statements of rhetorical grandiose to purport the accuracy of their assertions. Never will they objectively examine real life measure of American success and economic improvement like the Housing Affordability Index for example. The Housing Affordability Index measures whether or not a typical U.S. family makes enough money to just to qualify for a mortgage loan on a typical home let alone buy one. But this will never be included in their writings because data indicates that US housing affordability is at its lowest point since the fourth quarter of 2008. This most likely is a consequence of stagnate wage growth that cannot keep up with increasing home prices.

They may cite job creation as an indicator of Obama's success but will go no further than the Whitehouse press statement to examine the fine details of the data, for if they did, as a new study by economists from Harvard and Princeton note, nearly 95% of the ten million new jobs created during the Obama era were part-time or temporary positions. I won't even include that additional analysis of liberal media pundits will not note or question how many of these new jobs are being taken by people that already have a job or even two. In all accuracy, since Obama took office, there remains 1 million fewer workers, overall, working than before he took office (another actor to consider when attempting to comprehend why US housing affordability is so low and wage growth so paralyzed).

In simple terms, although Obama did inherit an economic mess, his policies have led to deteriorating affordability in home ownership, a segment of the U.S. economy that traditionally has proffered parents with the best opportunity to safeguard a better future for their children. Instead, his Keynesian economic approach has added another obstacle for lower-income Americans regardless of race. I mean, the housing market bubble burst almost 10 years ago, yet sales and construction in this sector are well below their peaks in the early 2000s meaning the housing sector is stagnate along with wage growth.

Thus to abrogate the use of data, anything is not only open to vapid complaints by democrats but is also the fault of the man who has not even been sworn in as president yet. This is the ultimate profile of the traumatized individual. This can be made even worse for progressive peace-loving democrats when we include Obama's foreign policy record.

When Obama took office he vowed to end the war in Afghanistan. This too has not happened and to use the same language pundits use to describe the statements of Trump, was a lie. Not only has he increased military operations in

Afghanistan, he has dropped more bombs, employed more drone killings than Bush, and has killed inordinate more innocent civilian in the country when compared to his predecessor. Then there is Libya and Yemen. The 2009 Nobel Peace Prize winning PresidentAdministration has sold more weapons than any other American president since World War II, totaling plus $200 billion from 2008 to 2015. Sales to Saudi Arabia alone has swollen to $115 billion. Now he has sent US Special Forces to Lithuania to saber rattle on the Russian border.

Democrats and in particular Obama, really do see Donald Trump's election victory as a personal repudiation of his pluralistic and globalist agenda and legacy. Add to this that democrats need to not only figure out how to have policy messages that include all instead of dividing the nation in to mutually exclusive voting blocs based on labels and message of race, gender and sexuality, they also have to figure out how to formulate new integrative domestic policies with how to communicates those policies with a single unified message for all (and this can't be done by just speaking at colleges, universities, unions and big cities).

The democrats understand that what they have to stand on are Obama's past eight years and the political agenda of the democratic elite. While murder rates in traditionally democratic cities like Chicago, Memphis, Baltimore and DC are out of the atmosphere, they are doubling down. By some estimates, the Obama Administration and sanctuary cities and their mayor including in NYC, San Francisco and Chicago spend around $113 billion on illegal aliens annually but they ignore that there are U.S. citizens that can use these funds including but not limited to homeless veterans, our inner cities, our youth and/or rural areas, all being poor black and white folk alike.

Yes the Democrats have their own battle of Ia Drang Valley and they cannot see for the Elephant grass and are taking fire from all sides yet responding by shooting in all directions and at anything that moves from a Simon & Schuster book deal for Milo Yiannopoulos, to the HBCU band from Talladega College performing at the inauguration to GM CEO Mary Barra being appointed to Trump's business Advisory council (yet don't mention how Obama pimped US tax payers for GM), to Putin, WikiLeaks and so-called 'fake news'. They have been dropped off in the middle of their own Landing Zone X-ray and do not know what to do. They never look at themselves to determine if their battle plan was defective yet instead blame everything else. But now they have run out of replacement parts for the Iroquois "Huey" helicopters that carried them into battle and are running out of ammunition and have few if any reinforcements arriving for some time. The Battle of the Ia Drang Valley was one of the most noteworthy battles of the Vietnam war, likewise, the battle the Democrats have on their hands after the 2016 presidential election loss, will be just as significant.

The Failure of Marx and Engels

After the recent election, I started to wonder about how we actually got to where we are. In this process I was reminded of two individuals in particular, Karl Marx and Frederick Engels. These came to mind because there seems to be either a sentiment or Marxism or socialism arise in the U.S. that in my life time I have never experiences or noticed. I say both because I am not sure as to which one it is: social conflicts in relationships between different classes of people as an impetus for future egalitarian social transformation (Marxism), or questions regarding whether or not all means of production, distribution, and exchange should be owned or regulated by the collective members of the U.S. as a whole (Socialism).

This is not a holistic interpretation, but rather singularly relegated to political objectives of the American progressive left.

Marx and Engels met in the 1840s if my history is correct, in industrial Germany. Back then it was either called Prussia or Bavaria. They connected due to their mutual appreciation for the philosophical writing of Hegel. For the laymen, Hegel, although known for many contributions to philosophy, one of his most interesting propositions he introduced was the Hegelian dialectic. The Hegelian dialectic was how in his view, all of human history unfolds; specifically that history progresses as a dialectical in the form of thesis, antithesis, synthesis.

Now I won't go into dialectical materialism, but to put in basic terms, Marx and Engel used the Hegelian dialectic to describe their philosophical views of social systems in terms of the capitalist economy as a function of man's progression to an eventual socialist/communist state. Their argument was that in the future, capitalism would become obsolete and end (be destroyed by the worker class). They detailed this concept in the *Communist Manifesto*. They believed that with the introduction of industry, and the business owners' desire for more and more wealth accumulation (capital), the only outcome left would be that the worker would never benefit, would only grow greater in number and be more concentrated in mass in industrial areas of production. This would be the new and final stage of social existence and an end to the unequal relationships between different social classes (for the worker class would link together and eventually revolt against the owner class to address what they perceive as unfair with the manner in which our international economic system operates and correct the dysfunctional social order).

Honestly, don't see too much Hegel in their economic philosophy. After all, they seem to have one supposition and stuck with it whereas Hegel postulated that there are gradations of reality within various phenomena, meaning his original commentary endorsed that there can be degrees of truth in proposals. Hegel specifically indicated in *The Phenomenology of Mind* that there exist both material and mental phenomena.

Although the *Communist Manifesto* seems to be an attempt to explain the goals of the theory behind Communism, by speculating that the exploitation of one class by another is the motivating force behind all historical developments, they fail to integrate aspects of the human condition, or of those intangible activities of the basal ganglia and prefrontal cortex of each human that make us the unique species we are. Marx and Engels assert that capitalism will be transformed in the direction of socialism, yet they ignore the human effects of cognition. They obviate differences in races and gender in their outcomes albeit biology dictates distinctions in cognitive function based on gender for example. They fail to include that the collective unconscious (and for the record I despise Jung) of man may or may not forget their past, if it was historically filled with events of trauma based on race. This is consistent with language also, for we define and see our world according to how we understand our environment via language. These distinctions are important and may reflect what Hegel described as the "lacerated consciousness."

I say this because one of the goals of Marxism is cultural – cultural Marxism being a form of social engineering that through political correctness (for lack of a better term), seeks to obviate capitalism and class structure because it is oppressive, by destroying traditional the concepts of family, morality, race, gender and sexual identity. This is achieved by cultivating a single victimized group solidified to fight the capitalist oppressors. For Marxists/socialist, this is mandatory to fulfill their societal goals.

If this is the objective, then Marx and Engels have failed. The failure is because they never consider that all groups, albeit they adopt standards of political correctness and promote their status a victims openly as a collective, will eventually lean towards expressing their human condition in terms of their mental phenomenological experience more so than their collective material phenomenological experience. No clearer can this (to bring me back to my original reflection) be observed on this eve of the inauguration of Donald Trump as the 45th President of the United States of America. Plans are inthe works for thousands of journalists, academics, intellectuals, entertainers,and other leftist progressives to protest and make lucid their objection and rejection of the President Elect in the name of preventing America from becoming fascist. If they succeed they will be happy but it will be the end of Marxist/socialist ideology in America, for they will fall back into their personal ascribed states of victimhood, rather based on gender identity, race, ethnicity or ethnic affiliation. And when this happens the conditions of man that Marx and Engels excluded from their theory – the nature of man, will bring them back to man's primal class system, one of good versus evil.

Obama's China and Russian Foreign Policy Hypocrisy

As the Obama Administration prepares to leave the Whitehouse, a major contradiction in his policy approach when comparing Russia with China exist. From hacking to perceived military threats it appears that there are two standards involved in President Barack Obama's decision making.

Although with respect to China and the sparing pertaining to who will control the waterways of the South China Sea (a waterway through which trillions of dollars in oil, gas and other trade go through annually) or the massive Office of

Personnel Management (OBM) hack, we as a nation have taken no actions similar in magnitude as we have with Russia based on opinions and beliefs regarding alleged hacking of private individuals and corporations when compared to China. Why?

Unlike with Russia and their moves around the Balkans and with the Ukraine, in which the U.S. has engaged in war games and recently amassed hundreds of military vehicles and thousands of troops, the Obama administration has softened the drama of the Navy missions through the South China Sea by insisting that the U.S. is just traveling through international waters.

Like China, Russia actively seeks to avoid a direct conflict with the United States. However unlike Russia, China's saber rattling is loud, very loud and Beijing is sending its messages, brash messages for the Obama administration in many forms, rather it be building up military installations in the Spratly Islands or the Scarborough Shoal in the South China sea, expanding their strategic footprint in the Asia-Pacific region, or their growing investment in expanding and modernizing their military. But what did the Obama Administration do? Nothing. At least when compared to the ephemeral threat that Russia fosters, they required war game maneuvers on the edge of its borders.

The U.S. sees the South China Sea as international waters. However from President Obama to National Security Advisor Susan Rice, given the importance the administration states, it merits no response at all. But it can only be expected for their response to the massive hacking into the OBM by China engendered a similar lack of response. When the Obama administration openly acknowledged that the Chinese frequently attempts to steal American trade secrets and considers such actions as acts "of aggression" no diplomats were expelled. This although we know that the Department of Homeland Security and the Department of the Interior have evidence that indicates several networks were compromised by hackers in the OPM's and Interior's networks by state sponsored Chinese actors. More than 20 million federal employees were exposed including military and intelligence personnel by simple "doxing" by allegedly a cyber-espionage group including but not limited to data on retirement plans, work schedule, finger prints and personal identifying data. Sadly from networks with problems in security and weaknesses that were known of and had existed for the tenure of the Obama Administration. Especially given that these older systems (that are written in COBOL) couldn't be updated to support encryption. Even more comical is that the Chinese use simple Windows Power Shell attacks to insert remote access tools (RATs) on Windows desktops and servers .

But even with evidence, the current Administration did not expel Chinese diplomates nor retaliate on the record openly as was the case with Russia. It seems (as illogical as it is) that the administration of President Barack Obama is both hesitant and wary to do anything that might instigate an armed conflict with China. Although we know that doxing (sending out private or identifiable information about an individual or organization via malware) is more severe than spear-phishing (trying to get dumb fcks to volunteer by clicking on an unknowing malicious link to extract sensitive info like usernames, passwords, and/or credit card particulars), the Obama Administration did zilch.

All we do with respect to Beijing is to allow them to operate in the South China Sea while we just talk shit. When the Navy or the Pacific Command say check them Chinese tricks Obama be like naw, don't be tripping. Even when China scrambled fighter jets to track U.S. ships in the South China Sea Obama say it ain't no biggie - and don't mention or add them Chinese ICBM test.

Honestly, I feel a war with Beijing is more a likely outcome than one with Russia. But instead of making preemptive military moves against China, we send tanks and other equipment to Germany to move them deeper into Eastern Europe, including more than 3,000 US soldiers in Poland and additional troops in Norway. Obama states that his actions are in response to Russia's intervention in Ukraine and to comfort NATO allies. This is questionable given President Obama's decision to waive legal restrictions on US provision ofdefense articles to allies in Syria by sending MANPADS to Syrian opposition forces.

Obama's deployment of troops in Europe is the largest US military fortification we have seen likely since the Reagan Administration. His position is that he needs to show a position of strength against Putin, as well as respond to unproved tampering in US elections. The problem is that there was no hacking in U.S. elections, rather hacking if it happened at all, into the email account of a private citizen whom emailed his password which was "password" and a private corporation – the Democratic National Committee. More importantly, the argument seems to be giving the American people more information about Hilary Clinton, her campaign and the DNC, is a threat to our democracy when I would assert otherwise. Is the administration suggesting that the American people didn't need to know as much as possible about the Clinton machine and that we would be better served know less? I hope not, for that, in addition to Obama's foreign policy inconsistency is a much greater threat, especially seeing that he is doing such on his way out of office.

Is Iraq and Turkey About To Bump Heads, For Real?

While many of us on this side of the pond have either been crying and complaining, or celebrating and enthusiastic due to the election of Donald Trump, there's one thing we can all count on – the lack of mainstream media coverage on what is happening in Libya, Yemen and Iraq. I would add Syria, but the mere mention of Aleppo given the incessant repetition it is written and orally stated daily, makes me want to throw-up.

It seems that the Iraqi security forces, elements of the Iranian Republican Guard, Shia militias and Kurdish Pesh-merga, after more than three months, have ISIS jihadist on the ropes and are finally entering Eastern Mosul, closing in on ISIL/ISIS last positions. To be succinct, the battle has been more of an effort and struggle than the Obama Admin-istration said it would be since the Mosul offensive began October 17. At one point the United Nations had reported that more than 2,000 Iraqi troops had been killed by Novem-ber (a figure disputed by the Iraqi government and Iraq Joint Operation Command). According to the UN, this includes the army, police, Kurdish Peshmerga, interior ministry forces and pro-government paramilitaries.

At that time, it was reported that Iraqi troops had been the target of 630 suicide car bomb attacks in the first 45 days of the operation alone. The last report of US troop deaths was in November with 16 killed and 27 wounded. Although during that period the US Department of Defense only admitted to there being just a single casualty. Needless to say, both have ended reporting on military causalities as a result of the Mosul offensive.

It is hard to fathom that the Obama administration or the Pentagon did not conceive that recapturing Mosul would not be an easy task in particular given waiting more than two years of ISIL rule to do so and offering advanced notice of the operation. With the unexpected difficulty of uprooting ISIL/ISIS/Daesh fighters, and the more than anticipated length of time it has consumed thus far to do such, another problem has arisen that was not projected – a riff developing between Iraq and Turkey.

The Iraqi PM Haider al-Abadi is firmly and openly demanding that Turkish forces leave Bashiqa camp near Mosul. Turkey on the other hand has stated that they will not withdraw its troops from its Bashiqa military camp in northern Iraq until the Mosul offensive against ISIL/ISIS/Daesh is complete. To make their intentions even more clear, Turkey's defense minister Fikri Isik, in November said that their military participation was part of its groundwork for other and more "important developments in the region." This is a moot point for the Iraqi PM who indicated that any efforts of diplomacy with Turkey could "not move forward one step" unless all Turkish forces in northern Iraq withdrew.

I am not certain but it would not surprise me that if Turkey, after the attempted Coup and still in the process of culling members of the military andgovernment, was really interested in preventing the Kurdistan Workers' Party (PKK) from establishing a solid link in the region in which they already have large population of Kurds in Turkey and Iraq. Erdogan May also be concerned that this might result in to a stronger diplomatic relationship with the PKK and Iraqi Shia Popular Mobilization Forces (PMF). This is something he cannot allow.

The Kurdistan Workers' Party is based in Turkey and Iraq. Since 1984 the PKK has waged an armed struggle against the Turkish state for equal rights and self-determination for the purpose of forming their own independent nation state. From this point of view, if I were Erdogan, this would be a tactic that could be employed to prevent the PKK elements from gaining a foot print in Tal Afar, an invalid fear according to according to the Iraqi's since they have guaranteed that PMF fighters will not get involved in the Mosul and Tel Afar campaigns.

Tel Afar, is a city and district in the Nineveh Governorate of northwestern Iraq. The leadership in Baghdad has vowed to defeat all "foreign troops" in and around Sinjar,

PKK and ISIL included. However, a senior representative of one of the many the Shia militias fighting ISIL in concert with the Iraqi government has warned that they are willing to use force against Turkish troops in Nineveh if the Turkish government refuses to withdraw from the area. Jawadal-Tleibawi, a high-ranking leader of the al-Hashd al-Shaabi militia said in press statements said that if diplomacy fail, his fighters are "capable of forcing out the Turkish occupiers" and called the actions of Ankara as "a flagrant intervention in Iraq's domestic affairs".

Baghdad has described Turkish military presence in Iraq as a violation of its sovereignty, yet both openly indicate they a committed to meeting in the future to discuss a yet to come withdrawal plan pertaining to Turkish troops in the country. Although Turkey has retained the importance of their troop deployment in the area, they equally prioritize both the importance of training local militias to combat Islamic State militants and reducing the influence of Kurdish PKK militia operating in Iraq. Moreover, Ankara is openly precarious of al-Hashd al-Shaabi's involvement in Mosul battles, worrying that the predominantly-Shia forces could commit human rights violations against Sunni inhabitants (a concern that has been documented by Amnesty International and Human RightsWatch).

What has been made clear by Baghdad is that the Bashiqa camp is an Iraqi camp has to and will be run and controlled by Iraqi administrative authorities. However a recent visit by a visit to meet Turkish troops by Turkish Health Minister Recep Akdağ and Energy Minister Berat Albayrak to Bashiqa has stirred the pot even more and has troubled the Iraqi government. Iraq and Turkey have agreed that the Turkish military will withdraw from the Bashiqa camp when the Mosul offensive is complete, but until then, Baghdad wants the camp to immediately be turned over to Iraq control. Then there is Turkey's ultimatum that Baghdad end any and all financial support to local groups in the Sinjar region which they state are affiliated with the PKK.

Whatever the case is, even if ISIL is defeated and removed from Mosul, there will remain a major issue to be settled between the leadership in Ankara and Baghdad. Will it be settled peacefully with diplomacy or violently taking these two nations to the precipice of war is the query.

Next Up, The Netherlands and France

I would love to be a fly on the wall at Davos. I can only imagine the panic filled discussions being had over not just Brexit, but also the defeat of Hillary Clinton. All of their plutocratic wealth accumulation schemes at the expense of the common person, and neoliberal plans of incessant domination as of now, look for them to be a giant ice cream cone that is melting before their eyes and in their hands due to the heat of populism. Even when they leave their luxurious surroundings in the snow-peaked Swiss Alps at the annual World Economic Forum, they will continue to have nightmares and dreams of what could have been because of what is up next at the plate.

Within the next eith weeks the Dutch general election will happen on March 15. As it stands, the current front runner and favorite is the leader and founder of the Dutch Party for Freedom (PVV) Geert Wilders. The PVV has been described as being far-right and anti-Islam with Wilder himself recently being tried (for hate speech) in court, accused of inciting hatred against Moroccans. His crime was asking a crowed at a rally in 2014 if they wanted "fewer or more Moroccans in your city and in the Netherlands". After the throng began to shout "fewer, fewer," he responded: "We're going to organize that." Although the resulting verdict found Wilders guilty of inciting discrimination, his views and support has only grown. Like Trump, he is seen as an anti-establishment firebrand who speaks the language of the people and tells it like it is.

Pundits have projected that the PVV could win as many as 35 seats this year which would make it the majority power in the 150-seat Dutch parliament. Present policy positions presented by the PVV include but are not limited to closing down all Islamic schools and mosques, shutting down the borders, a complete ban on migrants from Islamic nation states, banning the Koran and calling for a referendum on Dutch EU membership in a hope to pull the Netherlands out of the 28-nation institute, should he become prime minister. Thus it is not improbable that the Christian Wilders, with his promise to start a complete "de-Islamification" of the Netherlands, could become the country's next Prime Minister.

After the Dutch elections, in April and May the first and second rounds of the French presidential elections will take place, and like the Netherlands, the far-right has a strong chance of winning. As it stands, Marine Le Pen of the National Front is just a few points ahead of her conservative rival and former front-runner François Fillon of Les Républicains party based on recent surveys conducted by Ipsos Sopra Steria for Sciences Po University Research Centre (Cevipof) and Le Monde. In the past French voters have supported the National Front to the runoff stage of elections; however this was when the current candidate's father was running. This time it will be after both the election of Donald Trump and the Brexit vote. Like Obama, the French reflect a similar level of disappointment for both François Hollande and his predecessor Nicolas Sarkozy. Trump's anti-NAFTA rhetoric is similar to the position of Le Pen regarding the European Union trying to establish a free-trade zone across Europe and North America that would be called the Transatlantic Free Trade Area (TAFTA).

Like Trump and Wilders, Le Pen boasts a similar form of political nationalism. She has been extremely critical of the migration policy of German Chancellor Angela Merkel and has ceaselessly indicated her desire, being labeled a Eurosceptic, to take France out of the EU and/or euro seeing she has pledged to hold a referendum on France's membership in the organization. In addition she holds views some have described as being anti-Islam. For example, she believes that the children of illegal immigrants should not have access to French public schools. In concert with president Trump, she is for working closer with Russian President Putin and sees the utility of NATO as being questionable. In one recent interview with the BBC she was quoted as stating, "NATO continues to exist even though the danger for which it was created no longer exists."

Whatever the result, a Le Pen win is set to usher in a new age of right-wing politics for France after decades of centrism. With the UK removed, along with Germany there remains only France to hold the top positions of power in the EU as nation states. And for this to continue, Le Pen and her far-right party would have to fall in defeat to her center-right opponent. If not a Le Pen victory could mean the end of Europe as we know it.

If France's Marine Le Pen and the Netherlands' Geert Wilders were to become president and Prime Minister of their respective nations, the impact of their victories would likely be felt far beyond Europe, especially with elections on the horizon in Germany. Not only could it result in a domino-effect of Brexit-style referendums in other member nations, it may entrench the observation that globally in the west, the mistrust of established corporate, media and political elites will continue to display itself in a tug of war between populist and establishment forces. Also, it will signal that more policies that are anti mass immigration, anti-austerity and anti-EU may not be too far behind.

Neoliberal detractors may say that politicians like Trump, Le Pen and Wilders are exploiting a populist agenda by capitalizing on irrational beliefs and views. Unfortunately the reality is that people are sick and tired of not having their political, or any interest represented by the contemporary status quo and feel they are not being represented by, or benefiting from current dysfunctional,neoliberal or neoconservative mainstream policies. They have seen what has happened in Greece and the impact that mass immigration and migration policies can have on a nation's security and serenity. They are seeing increasing levels of terrorism once where they had not and are experiencing little and little less in their wallets and purses to even meet their basic needs. Even more sad and offensive is that mainstream politicians and most journalist not only are not trying to understand these phenomena but rather ignoring them as if a passing fad.

So if the Netherlands and France are next to follow Trump and Brexit, it could significantly damage the dream of a single unified shared economy for the Eurozone and significantly weaken the European Union as a world power and more importantly, signal that populist movements will continue to cultivate in Europe and the progressive left and other traditional supporters of neoliberalism will remain behind the curve or on the outside looking in.

Manufactured Synthetic Outrage

The veil of hypocrisy is best seen when one looks in the mirror. It is opaque and empty until we accidentally see it while we are putting on our makeup, or a tie to adorn our image. Our hypocrisy is so consistent, especially here in America that it should be used like a scientific constant similar to Planck's or Avogadro's number.

It seems as that President Trump's recent announcement of a temporary ban on immigration from several specific countries got a lot of folk upset, 99 percent of them who presented no real outrage to the policy or even the ban, but rather the man who implemented it. They are out in mass protesting at airports on behalf of these individuals as if their life depended on it. Now I too disagree with Trump's implementation but not the policy. But unlike most, I am rational and have been consistent, in my views from president to president, but I will never evince the fake and cosmetically contrived outrage band wagon revolutionaries show whenever they get their feelings hurt or do not get their way.

It is comedy at its best and more life-like than anything Hermippus or Eupolis could have ever written. And I say this honestly, because although I have been pained by the refugee crisis for more than six years now, I was more upset at the Obama administration for its continuous bombing and destruction of these humans homes and murdering their families, for creating this outcome from Libya to the South Sudan and equally the lack of concern partisan progressive neoliberals, allowed him to carry out his inhuman slaughter without protest.

You see, when Obama was droning weddings in Afghanistan, or providing Saudi Air force with targeting direction to drop US supplied cluster bombs and White Phosphorus on schools, hospitals and Yemeni markets using US F-15s, few of the many at the airports across American cities currently said a single world. Since it was Obama, it was "all good." Even still, there was nothing said when in 2011, then President Barack Obama and the Clinton state department stopped processing Iraq refugee requests for six months imposing a similar ban as Trump's. I say similar because if you take the time to read the EO (as I have) it is nothing like these idiot pundit talking heads describes it as being. Instead, they play the herd-like public, so distraught with emotional indignity and desecration so eager to accept what they see from TV without question. A more accurate representation of the EO is that it specifically focuses in on Syrians (Iraq, Iran, Libya, Somalia, Sudan and Yemen are not even declared, stated, cited or listed in the EO specifically). If they were, we can thank the past administration for this policy shift for these visa restrictions for these seven nations exactly, which was put in place by the Obama administration in 2015 for cats who had been in said nations after 2011 (ironically it was in March 2011 when a multi-state NATO-led coalition began a military intervention in Libya and at the same time the Obama administration instigated the civil war in Syria).

The only mention of the other nations are as follows: "For the next 90 days, nearly all travelers, except U.S. citizens,traveling on passports from Iraq, Syria, Sudan, Iran, Somalia, Libya, and Yemen will be temporarily suspended from entry to the United States." It also goes on to state: "I hereby proclaim that the entry of nationals of Syria as refugees is detrimental to the interests of the United States and thus suspend any such entry until such time as I have determined that sufficient changes have been made to the USRAP to ensure that admission of Syrian refugees is consistent with the national interest."

If you read the NY Times, Wall Street Journal, Washington post (and I can only imagine mainstream TV/cable news), all I am seeing is messaging pushing the narrative that seven mostly Muslim nations are targeted from entering the US over the ninety day period. But this isn't true. Don't believe me, again read the EO yourself.

So when Democrats like Chuck Schumer and Elizabeth "full-blooded Indian" Warren, or media pundits whom proclaim to be objective journalist yet clearly do not know how to read or either comprehend processes that allow for the extraction of semantic meaning from words, express their

OFFENDEDNESS at President Trump's action, I have to question their sincerity, as I do with all these protestors.

I question if they care so much, then where have they been and why have they been silent. As I noted earlier, they didn't mind when Obama did it for a period of 120 days, nor complained when upon leaving office ending a privilege bestowed among Cuban migrants and immigrants of being allowed to enter the U.S. without a visa—and to remain with benefits. They were uncommunicative and closed-mouth even prior to this for when Obama approved policy designed to destabilize governments (neoliberal interventionism), allow for the bombing countries (undeclared wars of aggression), and arming jihadist extremists , no one complained then even when we saw the massive outflow of people from Niger, Sudan, Somalia, Eritrea, Libya, Iraq, Afghanistan and Syria among others. If you never complained about the Obama administration accelerated/enhanced drone policy, you are really in no moral or ethical position to complain about Trump's refugee policy. Look in that mirror and ask yourself, what's worse: Trump not allowing refugees to enter the US or Obama droning and bombing these peoples' into oblivion and creating an environment for fundamentalist cats that cut off heads, enslave women and girls, and burn people alive in an effort to control their communities? But no now we have a responsibility to refugees.

It is nothing wrong with caring and having compassion for others, but when it is phony and falls along partisan lines it borders on fascism. Such hypocrisy has no moral footing to stand unless you are willing to take these migrants in your home or have refugee camps built across from where you live, but I doubt you have that much care and sincere interest to go that far. I mean we have homeless people right here in America who many of the anti-Trump protestors drive past, don't help and even lock their doors and roll up their windows when they approach their car. Take San Francisco for example. Liberal democrats all over the city protesting for affordable houses but when plans were made to put that housing in their liberal democratic neighborhood they fought and still are fighting against it. I guess it is okay to protest for affordable housing for the poor and homeless as long as it isn't put next door to me

Clearly these protesters like to say it is an all-out Muslim ban when fact dictates these nations only account for 12 percent of all Muslims in the world – nations that have had similar bans against Israel but proffered no protest. But this is cool, but some aspects are not. For example, Starbucks announced it plans to hire 10,000 refuges but when it comes to former inmates or young black youth in America, they are content with them remaining unemployed. But like I said before, where was this activism when Obama & Hillary were creating refugees by dropping bombs on the homes they once owned in the places in which they hail from? And don't forget about the celebrity Hollywood cats that politicize the #Muslimban yet never mentioning that in the majority of their movies they portray Muslims as terrorist (which can be interpreted as progressives protesting under the claim that they are tolerant, but they are not). Tolerance for them only means accepting views comparable to theirs for reason and compassion is thrown out the window when you disagree with them. One can only speak your mind if you tow the same ideological line.

Something must change, it is as if you don't agree with someone, instead of listening and using reason and pragmatism, folks would rather just yell, call names and argue. This isn't productive. I will not point fingers but there is enough hypocrisy to go around feed the world indefinitely. Strange there's so much outrage over Trump's refugee ban compared to Obama's disastrous regime-change policies in Libya, Syria and Yemen. I know what trump did was idiotic, stupid and in American but for you fake outrage and not put in work in your back yard is equally stupid. This is what I meant by such being comical for the hilarity of the herd mentality cannot be ignored. And this is sad because as one writer pointed out describing all of the anti-Trump protest: "...marchers aren't waiting for the policy fog to lift. Their anger is directed at people, not policies. [These] protests [are] intended,above all, to express the protesters' moral superiority to the president and those who voted for him.... Why complain now, when no decision has been made? It delegitimizes the future protests and exposes the bias of the opposition. . . .An opposition focused on personality."

I just ask, is this you? Are you as loud when Israel already has a wall?

American Bolshevik

Long time ago during World War I, some cats in Russia started to show their disdain for the ruling aristocracy. Led by Vladimir Lenin, these leftist revolutionaries called themselves the Bolsheviks. By all accounts of the historical record, there was merit to their actions insofar as Russia had been under imperial rule for almost 200 years. The Bolsheviks represented the Russian Social-Democratic Workers' Party who supported political change by any and all means including militarism. They promised their followers that they would redistribute the land and wealth to address the massive income inequality of their time and by doing such, improve the conditions of all in the working class. Through massive protest, strikes and vandalizing property of the state and ruling class, ultimately Nicholas II was forced to abdicate, ending centuries of czarist rule. Eventually, in 1917 Lenin rose to become basically the dictator of the first Marxist state in the world.

Today in the United States, the facade of a similar nature is on the rise. Strange as well, the foundation for this outrage is neither grounded in reason or logic but rather pure emotions – emotions of hate and dislike for the newly elected President of the United stated of America Donald Trump. I say this for like the Bolsheviks or most movements grounded on singular ideology, the U.S. modern progressive left are so caught up on their beliefs and what they believe that they never consider the beliefs, views and perspectives of others without their views as being valid. It is for them binary – all or none, my way or no way at all there for I am legitimate and justified to take any action I desire. Just as with the divides between the Bolsheviks prior to 1917, they spend more time yelling and protesting than actually trying to communicate or get their beliefs out to the folk they claim to protest on behalf of.

And protest are effective, but how is one to know what they are protesting or desire to change if it is not conversed to the masses? How can such be effective if through social, mass and mainstream media outlets the visual relayed is burning buildings, smashing car windows and vandalizing property? How can it be communicated to the mass of citizenry who do not agree with you if you shut down first amendment rights such as free speech? Doesn't diversity in addition to race, ethnicity, gender and sexual orientation also include political views?

Liberal by definition means being open to new behavior or opinions and willing to discard traditional values. Thus a liberal university for example is by definition supposed to be an institution of higher learning that concerned mainly with broadening a person's general knowledge and experience as it pertains to the world around them, not just what they believe or feel comfortable around. One could not tell that this was the case operationally at the University of California Berkeley yesterday. UC Berkeley is supposedly one of the most "liberal" and "progressive" universities in America but I have learned that if one ascribes from a dissimilar opinion that the majority (mob) maintains (rule), you are not welcomed, disliked, threatened with violence and even worse not allowed to speak. Once upon a time, universities were places where all folk and anyone could sit down, talk and listen to each other without retribution. Not today. Now exchanging different perspectives may hurt someone's feelings to the extent they need a puppy to pet or a safe space; places where there is only one side to all topics, either you are right or wrong – no exceptions. And anyone that dares to obviate this unspoken code will be attacked and highly likely subjugated to violent retribution because the words spoken by anyone with a differing perspective than these cats are terrifying, in particular if these individuals think for themselves and form their own opinions. For if one has control of language and vocabulary and is well-read (the latter being not hard to be now days), you may actually persuade them to think differently which makes throwing rocks and setting fires a more acceptable expression for them when they disagree and are frightened.

The funny thing is that the Democrats do not even recognize that it is these such behaviors that have given America Trump and a republican controlled House and Senate. These actions in particular their intolerance is what has lost them state legislatures and governorship's nationwide. They believe that since they control music, Hollywood and other celebrity spheres of reality that they are the dominant mainstream ideology – this is maniacal and false. They compare Trump to Hitler but do not know Hitler was never elected to office by the German people. Instead that he was appointed to be Chancellor of Germany by Paul von Hindenburg and did not assume the position of President until 1934 upon the death of Hindenburg, making himself Fuhrer of

Germany when he combined the office of Chancellor and President.

Even more comical is that the people who are afraid of Trump are on the surface even more vile, bigoted and hateful that the man they claim to oppose for the very same reasons. So much so that it is not uncommon for members on the anti-Trump left to call for open murder as one woman recently did, who claims to be a pre-school teacher, saying it was time to start killing people, starting at the White House.

The Bolshevik and like-minded cultural Marxist have arisen in the United States and I fear they are here to stay. I just hope they do not take us to the same outcome of authoritarianism they yielded in Russia. It was alleged that Winston Churchill once stated: "The fascists of the future will be called anti-fascists," I guess he may have been spot on with that.

Cory Booker, Tom Price & Big Pharma

For decades now I have been saying that there was no difference between Republicans and Democrats and with the election of Donald Trump, no time since now has this even more clear. Sure folk will say that Trump is a Republican, but I dare anyone to show any ideological bent he has toward either party. If he is a Republican, then Bernie Sanders is a Democrat. But a more articulate example of this can be observed when one tries to make a distinction between the actions and policies of traditional partisans like Cory Booker and Tom Price.

For cats attentive to history, we must recall we have Thomas Jefferson and James Madison to thank for our modern day derivative of what are now considered Republicans and Democrats. Both these men founded the Democratic-Republican Party. It was founded by these men to serve as a challenge to the Federalist Party which was run by Alexander Hamilton in 1791. Hamilton at the time was Secretary of the Treasury and a significant player in the administration in America's first President George Washington.

Madison and Jefferson questioned Hamilton's interest in truly wanting America to be a republic since he sided with the concept of federalism and disapproved of the manner in which the Constitution was written to limit the government and not the people. In contrast, Jefferson and Madison claimed the Constitution gave the federal government too much power such that it might place the citizenry at risk of being oppressed if there was no Bill of Rights to guarantee individual liberty. As an outcome of this, the first two U.S. political parties were formed – the Federalist Party (Hamilton) and the Democratic-Republican Party (Jefferson).

These two parties did not last too long and by the twentieth century, there was just one party divided in half – the Democratic Party and the Republican Party. Both of which have decided their main objective is not to serve on behalf of the unalienable individual rights of the citizen but rather the mechanical apparatus of the national government . Moreover, instead of the business of the people, their goals, motivated by political avarice motioned toward personal enrichment by becoming a professional class – something the founding fathers feared when they desired citizen merchants to serve and eventually return to the community.

Seeing this truism in modern day partisan politics, there is no better example than the relationship between Tom Price and Cory Booker with big pharma. The record is clear on both these politicians and their relationship with large U.S. pharmaceutical giants. Price was the benefactor of large campaign contributions from a CEO whose company manufactured a drug with the shelf name of BiDil - A treatment for African Americans suffering from heart failure, although one study raised problems about its safety and effectiveness.

Add to this, the recent. Kaiser Health report that Price invested in an Australian biotech company named Zimmer Biomet which resulted for him a profit gain of more than 400 percent and may be even more profitable for the company with the enacting of the 21st Century Cures legislation Price supported. Likewise Sen. Cory Booker and 12 other democrat senators supported the same legislation which serves to lower drug safety standards. Booker also votedagainst the Sanders/Klobuchar amendment which would have allowed for the importation of pharmaceuticals from Canada and aided sugificantly in reducing the unreasonable and exploitive price gauging currently practiced by U.S. Pharmaceutical giants. Booker did this while remaining one of the biggest recipients of pharma, receiving contributions in excess of with $260,000. Is there a difference between these two politicians although one is a republican and the other a democrat?

Well to answer this we have to beat the bushes a little more. Tom Price, the Georgia Republican nominated by Donald Trump to become head of the Department of Health and Human Services, received additional contributions from the CEO of Atlanta based Arbor Pharmaceuticals LLC who bought the rights to BiDil. In return he sought to have the aforementioned study questioning the drug safety and effectiveness removed from the federal government website. It was effective. Emails show that an assistant to Price contacted the federal Agency for Healthcare Research and Quality multiple times regarding having the study taken off their website according to documents obtained by ProPublica. It should be noted that Arbor is headquartered in Price's district.

Similar to Price, Booker too seems to be in the pocket of big Pharma. He demonstrated his true colors (green and white) when he visibly stood in opposition to a Senate amendment allowing for the importation of pharmaceuticals into the U.S. that would have lowered the absurd cost for drugs that is a major economic burden on millions in the U.S. Considered to be a potential 2020 presidential contender, Booker's office issued a statement saying that he was in favor of the importation of prescription drugs but that "any plan to allow the importation of prescription medications should also include consumer protections that ensure foreign drugs meet American safety standards. I opposed an amendment put forward last night that didn't meet this test." This alone is questionable and goes against attempting to aid the tens of millions of U.S. Citizens struggling to deal with the exorbitant cost of prescription drugs because it is the same argument made by the Pharmaceutical Research and Manufacturers of America (PhRMA) and the Obama Administration prior. Not to mention that Democratic Sen. Ron Wyden amendment to the Sanders/Klobuchar legislation included a clause for verified safety certification.

So is there a difference between Republicans and Democrats on ideology? I Would say no and that the Democratic-Republican Party established by Thomas Jefferson and James Madison are mirror images of each other and represent a professional class that have the singular objective to enrich themselves at the expense of the American people.

2300 Pages of Nothing

One word I use frequently, well really two are hilarity and comical. So forgive me for I am about to employ their use again but this time it will be in reference to Dodd-Frank. Not the law itself but rather the outrage I have heard from people regarding President Trump's desire to review and possibly gut the bill. Trump has just outline his plan to revisit the legislation introduced by President Obama approaching some seven years ago. In light of this, I asked several people how they viewed his decision. And the comedy followed.

The first few people said straight up that this was a bad idea and that Trump was just messing up again. They were vehement in their positions so I probed more asking two questions: (1) can you explain the Dodd-Frank legislation to me, and (2) have you ever read the legislation? I was not surprised for as I had anticipated none of the four had ever read it nor could they explain the law. Why is it that people get outraged at things they really have no understanding or knowledge of?

In my own view, Dodd-Frank is a worthless waste of trees. It basically amounts to 2,300 plus pages of nothing. When President Obama signed Dodd-Frank into law he told all Americans that it would serve as a stimulus to the U.S. economy. Instead of taking his word for it, I spent a week reading and trying to understand as much as I could proffer about the law. I read a lot of rules included in the law, hundreds, so many that I could only conclude some redundancy and some inherent contradictions.

What was clear was that it would not do one thing: end the practices of the "too big to fail" banks that brought about the 2008 financial crisis. It did however, with all of the new regulations, grow the size and cost of government albeit it claimed to streamline the regulatory processes for Wall Street.

That was then and after the end of the Obama administration, the Government Accountability Office (GAO) has documented some of my initial concerns. Not only has it added thousands of new government jobs it also cost in excess of a billion dollars for the law to be implemented annually. Moreover, the largest U.S. financial institutions are still "too big to fail" and in most cases have grown into even larger than they were prior to Dodd-Frank becoming the law of the land.

In short, small business lending from banks has dropped dramatically and there are fewer smaller banks across the country, thus creating less competition among these institutions in the favor of bigger banks compared to smaller community banks. Moreover, since most small business and start-up happen at the local level, with fewer small community banks, there has been the consequence of fewer new business startups.

It may end up that Dodd-Frank could have made the U.S. financial system even more unstable than it was in 2008. Then there is the fact that the legislation did not address any of the issues prevalent with Fannie Mae and Freddie Mac, which can be considered the main catalyst for what occurred in 2008. One reason for this could be that the Obama administration focused on pushing that what led to the financial crisisin 2008 was a lack of oversight and regulation of the financial system. Although I am no economist, I would disagree with this assertion because there has always been oversight it was rather that regulators mainly came from the banks they were supposed to regulate and often either looked the other way when wrong doing occurred, given a slap on the wrist or in a worse case, gave big banks special treatment.

All in all, it can be said with substantial evidence that Dodd-Frank did not do what it said it would do. And not to say that I know what President Trump will do, I can say it does need to be looked at again, in particular in terms on how it inhibits new business formation and puts the federal government in bed with these massive financial institutions. I also don't like how it plays favoritism with big banks allowing them to borrow money at lower rates than smaller banks. Similarly the manner in which it allowed big banks to add a banking fee to anything has contributed greatly to the tightening of purse straps demonstrated by a large body of the U.S. populos. Before Dodd-Frank more than three out of four banks provided free checking, now this is a thing of the past and may be why more and more people either do not want or

can no longer afford to have a bank account. But like I started with, if you ask me, Dodd-Frank is worth less than the
paper it was printed on.

Puzzy Lemonade Outrage or Do Blacks Care About Any-
thing Besides Beyoncé?

Years ago there was a little girl, she operated a lemonade and
candy stand, her name was Heaven Sutton. She isn't with us
anymore because she was gunned down in her front yard.
Now years later the names of children killed by senseless
gangland (or any form) violence in places like Chicago are
too numerous to name. Acen King, Ja'Quail Mansaw, Cylie
and Caden McCullum, Payton Benson, Antonio Smith Jr.,
Tiana Ricks and Londyn Samuels are just a few, but you
don't know their names or even know who they are. They
were never romanticized with hashtags like #remeberher-
name or #sayhisname or #bringbackourgirls because although they were black there death's were not sensational
enough for the retro chic political narrative of the day.

If they were killed by police or an idiotic white luna-
tic, they would be known and remembered and we would cite
their names with the likes of Oscar Grant, Trayvon Martin or
Michael Brown. But they have no value in the eyes and
minds of social justice warriors because mentioning or re-
membering their names does not help to enable their goals of
getting rich off of racial and identity politics and obtain fake
fame by receiving television air time for pretending to be
"woke."

The artificial pretense of the so-called woke culture is
metastasizing like a cancer, especially with the election of
Donald Trump. It is as if black folk can only attend to complaining about him and police shootings and nothing more.
Not the pathetic state of our inner cities. Or our failing gov-

ernment public schools or increasing rates of poverty (all of which by they have been happening in places that have been run by democrats since the 1940s in most cases and problems Trump had nothing to do with). The fake outrage at the election of Donald Trump that I have written about before will never manifest into true honest civic outrage for real problems that confront us daily like the deaths of the little children or the economic constraints I mentioned previously.

These same folk, especially the black ones will protest against Trump and his ban on seven specific nations but were silent when Obama was bombing families of the same innocent women and children in the same nations with his drone wars which he dramatically increased when compared to George W. Bush after giving his 2009 Nobel Peace prize acceptance speech: wars that the former president conducted with impunity in places like Somalia, Libya, South Sudan, Afghanistan and Syria that created his current migrant-refugee crisis to begin with. They are loud when they are not allowed within the U.S. proper but were quiet when they were being slaughtered religiously on the orders of America's first black president. It is as if they say it is cool to kill them, I can get with that but it is a problem when we try to improve criterion for entry to the U.S.

For the life of me I cannot figure this out – being open to individual and personal acquiesce to murder but opposed to none murderous acts to an option of personal choice.   Likewise, there was no outrage when Obama stopped Iraqis from immigrating to the U.S. for 120 days. Clearly politics and not protest in the name of basic dignity is hey problem or issue.

At Berkeley we saw this in action. Incantations of divide and conquer. Destroying property and setting vehicles on fire has nothing to do with protest based on what is called for to stand on the side of righteousness regarding human dignity or else they would affirm the nonviolent approaches of Gandhi, King and Mandela. This is all show and mechanically contrived vexation. They do not really care, they just want attention; and they do not seek change, rather they only want to define what is acceptable or should be tolerated as meaning you have to agree with me or else you are wrong and my speech is more important than your speech. What I am paying attention too is more important than anything else. But where were they before this?

For example, cities and states all around the nation have been finding funds available to deal with litigious actions that may be pending for illegal aliens under asserted or proposed Trump planes to deal with the issue. You got black folk even out on the front lines of this fictitious battle. Mind you that for decades we have been trying to get the same cities and states to hire more public defenders for the many of our fellow men and women locked behind bars but the response was always "we do not have the money for such." Yet there were none of these adamant protestors standing next to us when we made this request but we stand with them. And all of a sudden places like LA can magically come up with $10 million for this but no funds for additional public defenders to defend people born in America.

It is as if we are living in an alternate reality where all injustices are equal when evidence dictates they are not. There were only one specific people designated as slaves in America who did not have a choice to come him but rather was forced to by a combination of the Bible and the barrel of a gun. Still opaquely innocent and manipulated we go along with the flow when it makes no logical senses and supersedes our own collective interest. We hail the arrival of Muslim immigrants without out the consideration of the fact that if they are terrorist, they will kill us too, and want to kill us too. Liberal or conservative they do not care, they will set you on fire and chop your head off with the quickness for things we call liberties (sexual orientation, wearing revealing clothing if you are a woman, drinking alcohol, being a Christian or having an abortion).

That they do like beating women and condemning homosexuals to death don't outrage us, nor what they believe. It is this myopia that believes we are justified not to speak up on behalf of the children I mentioned earlier because they do not meet our narrative. But don't let it be an award show, or you will have protest and outrage out the azz. There would be #oscarssowhite or the recent #grammyssowhite because Beyoncé didn't win album of the year. This is an issue although WORLDWIDE the woman she lost too sold waaaaaaaay more albums than she did. Now let that sink in, cats are so mad that a millionaire didn't win an award while sitting in a room filled with other millionaires outfitted in $5,000 or more worth of sartorial splendor, that they are willing to express emotional disdain. But let a two-year get shot in the head the result of a gangland hit, and they won't say jack. But it makes sense, after all these rich Hollywood cats are oppressed too, with their body guards with automatic weapons, drivers and walled-in mansions.

Have we lost our way? Are we so caught up in self-absorbed mindless celebrity twaddle that we can be eaisly paraded about like a puppet by presentations of what Juvenal called "bread and circuses?" Do we even know what we are upset by, angered by or protesting against? I don't think so and I don't think for those who are black, really have have any interest in improving our conditions collectively as a people, if they were, they would know of Lavontay White, Takiya Holmes or Kanari Gentry Bowers. Unfortunately they don't, they just know Beyoncé didn't win a Grammy for Album of the year and that it takes precedence above all else.

The Stasi Has Returned and it is American

The sudden resignation of National Security Adviser and retired General Michael Flynn and the unprecedented leaks pouring out to damage and even destroy the Trump presidency is a throwback to what I recall other nations (namely autocratic or communist regimes) did when the political status quo felt threatened. Likewise, they often emerged as a consequence of actions taken by top members in state sponsored intelligence operations.

There are several possibilities for this including oscitant retribution proffered by folk like former CIA director John Brennan and former acting CIA Director Michael Morell, or even a backlash by career officials (Democratic politicians and, more importantly, the intelligence community) in an effort for whatever reason, to keep Trump from instituting his foreign policy agenda.

Sadly many in the elite east coast press and large numbers of Democrats support these actions while failing to accept and admit that for unelected officials to go around the constitution and imped policy efforts of a democratically elected official, whether you support that official or not, is seditious and boarders on actions of former governments run by police apparatus like the Stasi of East Germany.

The Stasi was a shorthand term used to describe the East German State Security "Staatssicherheit." It was a combination of the United States FBI, CIA and NSA for lack of a better description, meaning they had policing, investigating and uninhibited surveillance powers. The Stasi was responsible for hundreds of thousands of perceived political opponents being tried without due process, imprisoned and even murdered in an effort to suffocate political dissention against all the tenants of conventional democratic standards.

Most people they imprisoned and executed where charged with specific acts such as engaging in "propaganda hostile to the state," interfering in "activities of the state or society" orthe "treasonable relaying of information." In addition to domestic surveillance, the Stasi was also responsible for foreign surveillance. Through the use of wiretapping (it is illegal to wiretap the U.S. President) and anonymous unsourced claims unaided by any evidence (sounds familiar), for more than four decades, the Stasi operated unfettered and without remorse until the collapse of Communist East Germany and the opening of the borders with West Germany in 1989. These type of energies seem to have been put into action inside the Beltway as it regards the Trump administration.

It is obvious that there is a real fear or hatred for Trump as he goes about his campaign promise to "drain the swamp" and dismantle the bureaucratic system of politics including the FBI, CIA and NSA and their historic abuse of unfettered power that they feels places them over the elected government. Also clear, is that even before Hillary Clinton ran, highbrow member of the Washington political establishment, including assets of the U.S. intelligence apparatus, were supporting her hook, line and sinker. From former acting CIA Director Michael Morell and Gen. Michael Hayden who served in the capacity of both director of the NSA and CIA under George W. Bush. Both men, without evidence or proof asserted that Trump was a "useful fool" and Russian agent being influenced by Putin.

Upon which, immediately rumors started to be thrown into the political ether. In particular when then candidate Trump continuously rejected the establishment narrative of the media and intelligence community that under the direct orders of Putin, Russia hacked the Democratic National Committee and Clinton campaign chair John Podesta emails in order to interfere with the election on the side and behalf of the Republican nominee. This was followed by a pile-on by the Democratic Party which since then have willingly encompassed this effort to disrupt the elected President who they gave no chance of winning.

Since then we have had the Trump "dossier" which was produced by a former member of the British intelligence agency MI6 and hired first by a never-Trump super Pac and then the Democratic Party to find some dirt on Trump. This report fell apart, although the media tried to establish a narrative that it was true, when it was proven that unlike the dossier stated as fact, Trump lawyer Michael Cohen had never secretly traveled to Prague in August to meet with Russian officials or had ever been to Czceh Republic..

Why would the intelligence establishment take this path? Well even a blind person can see that their preferences for Clinton was in line with all of their desired policy objectives: Trump wants to work with Putin to destroy ISIS and Clinton wanted to go deeper into Syria in an effort to get Assad out of office as she did Gadhafi in Libya. For this reason if my logic is tenable, targeting Trumps security executives would be paramount. More than likely, Flynn was planning to try and reform and change the mindset of the national security state in America. Such would have surly been an economic loss the military industrial complex could not afford to take a chance on. It has been said that all wars are banker's wars and we are well aware that banks dole out large sums of money to the US military and intelligence apparatus.

The short of the story is that the East Germany Stasi, even if not in body, in action is alive in the administrative halls of Washington, DC. Like the Stasi, elements in the U.S. intelligence community are essentially committing treason against the Office of the President of the United States by leaking classified material to the press. This is also without a doubt happening with the urging and assistance of former Obama administration appointees because anonymous leaks without any evidence at all is speculation, guessing and/or gossip. Unfortunately, the democrats and mainstream media flunkies are more than giddy to run with any claim, substantiated or not to bring down Trump and his administration. This is the most probably scenario given from the Obama years, we know the immense powers the U.S. intelligence community has through the leaks (not anonymous) of Edward Snowden alone and that he gave them even more powers days before leaving office. As one writer noted: "Selectively disclosing details of private conversations monitored by the FBI or NSA gives the permanent state the power to destroy reputations from the cloak of anonymity. This is what policestates do."

Any assertion regarding Russia's interference in U.S. elections as been presented based on guess and without evidence. The charges with Flynn began with the remnants of the Obama Department of Justice when then acting attorney general Sally Yates told the White House counsel that Flynn was not telling the truth with respect to talking about sanctions with the Russian ambassador. How did she know this and who authorized wiretapping Flynn's communication? Still, we do not know if this was true since the phone transcripts have not been released. All I can state is that these attacks against the President and his administration were planned and contrived in what I perceive as a hidden effort to thwart the will of the American people by elements representative of the Democratic Party, the U.S. intelligence establishment and mainstream media.

The Falsity of a Free Press

For some reason that I have failed to comprehend, people are actually up in arms over the manner in which President Trump is addressing and defining mainstream media outlets – namely CNN, the Washington Post, New York Times and MSNBC among others. I have heard it pronounced as an attack on democracy or that his actions characterize an effrontery to a free press. It is the latter notion that sets me aback for the press in America isn't reflective of free, rather it is corporatist for lack of an even more accurate description.

When we assert the concept of press freedoms or freedom of the press, it implies that there is no interference from any ever-powerful or omnipresent political or established state, or other organizational entity. We do not have this with the mainstream media in America anymore. What is called and referred to as a "free press" is in reality just a vehicle by which the public is fed the agenda of government and corporations under the cloak of unrevealed activities of elites in newsrooms primarily located in New York and Washington, DC. Modestly put, the mainstream media isn't a free press but rather a speaking board by which state and corporate bodies are able to repeat without investigation, the narratives designed to encourage spreading specific political information to program thought and behavior.

Moreover, the people that own and run these East and West coast news outlets are billionaires, like Rupert Murdoch, Michael Bloomberg and Amazon founder Jeff Bezos, who own all or significant proportions of media platforms the likes of the Washington Post, the Wall Street Journal and the New York Times. This is factual at the local level as well for Warren Buffett, the CEO of Berkshire Hathaway owns more than 60 daily newspapers across the nation. Taking this a step farther, it is estimated that 90% of what we watch, listen to and read is owned by 6 companies. Yes it is true, News Corp, Disney, Viacom, Time Warner, CBS and Comcast own 90% of the TV stations, radio stations, movies, magazines and newspapers that every American rely on for news, entertainment and information many require to be so-called 'woke.'

Such a consolidation of news media companies cannot be considered the stalwart of a free press, instead it is an 'owned press' in which freedom means motives of operation imbued in the content they select to provide or hide thanks mostly to Congress and the FCC, and which was accelerated in 1996 when then President Clinton signed the Telecommunications Act, which led to rapid consolidation of the radio industry. Just think about it, in 1983, 50 companies owned 90% of American media.

Now I know the contrarian who watches six or more hours of TV a day, well above the time we spend reading and asking questions will disagree. But history and the official record suggest otherwise. In 1975, the United States Senate Select Committee to Study Governmental Operations with Respect to Intelligence Activities found that the CIA submitted stories to the American press. In fact, in the 1950s, the CIA put in place Operation Mockingbird which was a program designed to, and effectively used US journalists at establishments like the New York Times and CBS to feed them official state propaganda stories to send out to their American consumers.

Journalists were even paid by the CIA to promote such stories or on the low end, just given the information and put it out as real news, when in fact it was made-up and fabricated propaganda - 'fake news'. The truth of the matter is that the US government via the CIA, has for years influenced US news media to advocate specific political storylines. Although Operation Mockingbird was supposedly ended in the 1970s, the objective and free thinking individuals could imagine that the Smith-Mundt Modernization Act of 2012 still serves the mission and purpose of the federal government by allowing for the American public to be a target audience for U.S. government-funded narrative inculcation campaigns. And don't sleep, it was way harder to carry out such activities after 1953 when Allen W. Dulles became director of the CIA because there were more individual players in terms of wire services and newspapers then.

I'm not sure but I think it was Malcolm X who called this shit 'tricknology'. These folk are effectively and actively trying to influence the narratives that mindless self-absorbed narcissist ignorantly consume in an effort to create your reality for YOU. And I know it is effective because YOU believe it. Wouldn't surprise me none if such cats watch the Oscars and see a movie about the White Helmets win yet yo dumb azz can't comprehend you been sold a storyline to completely hide the fact that the White Helmets are a component of Al-Qaeda. It is called TV programming and not TV reasoning – they just "programming" into your mind every single day for hours upon hours what they want you to think and accept without research and query to believe what they want you to believe and sway on how you see the world.

It is you, your bich azz that allow these immovable establishments to fix the agenda for what they want you to care about – Russians, Jeff Sessions and Russians, General Flynn and Russians, Russians interfered in out elections. But as I said, yet you don't even realize the information released in Podesta and DNC hacks (if the Russians released it or not) was accurate and factual but never ask if I should consider if I should have this information to make a electoral decision, or tow the MSM line that I should not use this to inform myself, although factual just because of what I watch on TV say you shouldn't? But keep on with the Bay of Pigs, Gulf of Tonkin, Mandela a terrorist, FBI didn't spy on MLK, there was not Tuskegee Experiment, we have to do Iran-Contra and the ubiquitous Iraq has weapons of mass destruction (when you knew Iraq never attacked us).

Six corporations' folk, ninety percent, send everything through your television, everything you watch. You can trust them folk, I won't. So wake up folk, can't be woke and sleep walking, they are not the free press, they got a pimp.

Obamacare: A Farrago of a Mess

On Monday, I read the transcripts from the Sunday morning talk shows. One comment that struck a tone with me that I read was from Laura Ingraham. Now honestly, albeit an intelligent person, I rarely agree with her observations but this time I did. She gave an apt description of Obamacare as a "libertine mess of a piece of legislation." I wanted to name this essay exactly this, however fearing copyright challenges, I came up with my own title of a similar nature

Regardless if you call it the Affordable Care Act or Obamacare, the fact is that for the vast majority of Americans, in particular the ones that lost coverage and now have higher premiums and deductibles, the foul side effects and unplanned imports have not been received well. Admittedly, no new government program is going to be completely perfect and however laudable a desire as it is to provide health insurance to millions that do not have any coverage, the reality is that health benefit mandates and willy-nilly rating rules significantly increase health insurance costs, and as a result are passed on to consumers.

I don't mind saying it, but I predicted all of this years ago. It began with, from the very start, when President Obama kept on saying that American families would experience an annual reduction of $2,500 in their health costs if his law was passed. This would be mathematically impossible unless some extreme assumptions could be made and they were. The biggest being one of structure given that the ACA doesn't even address the cost of health coverage. It is easy to make sweeping statements when the direct object of a statement (cost of health insurance coverage) isn't even spoken about in the legislation. Another and more problematic aspect of the law is that Obamacare can only work the manner stated if cats participate in the"individual mandate." If you don't then fear the tax and be fined either greater of 2.5 percent of your household's taxable income or $695 per uninsured adult and $347.50 per uninsured child in your family. This flat fee rate will increase each year with inflation. The assumption here was that if employer and employee insurance costs were greatly reduced, then that would have a direct, outcome on citizens in the form of the aforementioned $2500 per year for the average family. Maybe this is why then President Obama stated that his law would "not burden people who make $250,000 a year or less," or why he said that the ACA would not add "a dime" to the federal deficit.

None of what has thus far been presented has occurred. What has is that it has been estimated that the ACA will cost about $1.34 trillion over the next decade and that Obamacare's tax penalty connected with the individual mandate thus far falls more on lower-income and lower-middle-income individuals/families since subsidies for deductibles and other costs for income-eligible persons enrolled in the exchanges are available only to enrollees who select certain level health plans, which means that the plan must pay 70 percent of the average enrollee'stotal medical expenses for covered benefits. This in itself defeats the purpose of having insurance.

Economics side, another problem for many, myself included is that Obamacare abrogates individual and personal freedom not only by limiting choices but by allowing the government to make you to participate by buying insurance for not obeying the law. Almost every main decision in the health care sector of the American economy under the ACA is in the hands openly or ultimately, by federal officials – unelected federal officials.

But if you participate, you give up most of the liberty us as individuals connect with choice and medical freedom. Just take the Obamacare's Independent Advisory Board (IPAB) for example. This allows for the ACA to create a 15-

member panel of experts that determining the type of care that Medicare pays for on behalf of the individual and consequently rations Medicare through price controls for that individual – whatever they decide you are stuck with. Why, because under Title I, federal officials define the content of health insurance coverage, including but not limited to obligatory medical actions, treatment and preventive health care services. Then there is the large long-term care program called the Community Living Assistance Services and Supports (CLASS) Act. As early as five years ago we knew many of the components of the legislation were not practical or affordable. The Obama Administration's from the start knew that the CLASS act was not financially feasible, but wanted it and so kept the program anyway.

In summary, the ACA has increased costs for individuals,families, and businesses and unlike proponents of the bill claimed, instead the American people have come to hate the bill more and more. Not only is it worsening America's debt problem, federal spending on healthcare is also increasing which some believe will result in trillion-dollar deficits in seven years' time. The Congressional Budget Office has indicated that U.S. Federal debt could be as high as $30 trillion by 2030, as a consequence of Obamacare. Don't even include the absence of insurance options under Obamacare or the failing co-ops. Large insurance providers like Blue Cross Blue Shield, United Healthcare and Aetna are all leaving the exchanges and several states have only one insurer providing insurance through Obamacare. Less competition in the exchanges only means higher premiums and deductibles cost and less consumer choice (this is the law of supply and demand).

But such should have been expected, I mean congress had not even read the bill or given the chance to read the bill before being forced to vote on it. But folk still stick up for Obama care. But to me, a woman over 70 should not be forced to purchase prostate cancer or maternity coverage if she doesn't have a prostate gland and can't have a baby. But folk like this cat seem to don't get this. How would you feel if you paid the same price for auto insurance as a person with three DUI's? The ACA is truly a hodgepodge, mishmash jumble of confusion - a Farrago for lack of a better word.

Bush, Obama & Trump Middle East
Policy is One in The Same

I have attempted to stay out of the fray regarding what has just happened in Syria. It is almost as if Obama is still in Office and as if Trump has turned into Obama in the same fashion Obama turned into Bush. For all I know Trump is putting together a secret "kill list" like his predecessor and continuing Obama's drone strike assassination program. I have read some interesting perspectives on this topic and agree with many of them. For example, Norman Solomon's suggesting that all this incessant Russian bashing may have been used to 'bait' Trump to bomb Syria, with or without evidence. I also agree with MIT professor of Science, Technology, and International Security Dr. Theodore Postol in his assessment of the White House report noting that it provides no evidence that the Sarin came from or was dropped from an Airplane and that without being on the ground at the time such a position is impossible to prove given Assad's advantage in his battle against IS and other western supported terrorist proxies. For lack of a better statement, to use the words of Mike Whitney, "You don't have to be a genius to figure out that the case against Syrian President Bashar al Assad is extremely weak." Or as the free-thinking cats at MOA have pointed out, the White House "assessment" begins with "The United States is confident that the Syrian government conducted a chemical weapon attack..." noting that "the U.S....does not have"proof" - it is just "confident." And returning to Dr. Postol, he was also correct in 2013 when he disproved the Obama Administration uninformed position that Assad was responsible for a chemical nerve agent attack in Damascus. My question is will Trump be another Obama with respect to Foreign policy in West Asia and use his war powers even out there past Obama? Will he engage in even more unjustified and clandestine wars in the same way Bush and Obama did by targeting even more majority-Muslim countries?

Let us begin with some historical perspective. The west has had its eye on Syria for decades now. Although many would assert it started with a 1949 coup attemp implemented by the CIA just 3 years after Syria became an independent country, I would suggest it started after WW1 in 1919 and continued up until the Franco-Syrian war initially. Specifically, after the implementation of the Sykes-Picot Agreement in 1916 - which cut up what was left of the Ottoman Empire between France and Britain. The war itself happened in 1920 ending in a victory for the French and the formation of a new pro-French government. This resulted in Syria being divided in to several regions according to religion. This is an important historical event because it appears the object of current western interference and the call for regime change in the nation has a similar objective.

In addition, history shows us that the objective of these efforts was to dominate and control the rich natural resources (oil and natural gas) in the region. As early as 1957 President Eisenhower and British Prime Minister Harold Macmillan were making plans to establish and support financially the establishment of what they called a "Free Syria Committee" for the singular purpose of regime change in Syria to try and control the oil fields of not only Syria but also Iraq. There was no real geopolitical reason for this other than the desire of the Arabian American Oil Company (ARAMCO) to build a Trans-Arabian Pipe Line (TAPLINE) from Saudi Arabia to the Mediterranean via Syria through to Turkey. This required a "Syrian right-of-way" to be agreed upon without input from the Syrian people of course.

Unfortunately, the efforts of the west resulted in making a divide between Shiite and Sunni that has been going on since the seventh century even worse especially if one considers that Shiites are the majority in Iran and Iraq, and are the largest Muslim group in Lebanon and their lands include what many consider the richest oil fields in the entirety of the Middle East.

These efforts have only increased and intensified over the past few decades with regime change in Syria being priority. First a unified Syria stands in the way of policy objectives in the region to numerous and nuanced to discuss (US interests both in Lebanon and preventing the establishment of an Iraq's pipeline to the Mediterranean for example). We know this because recently unclassified documents show that the CIA even made plans to use Iraq, Israel and Turkey as proxies in 1983 to pressure the Syrian government by using covert military actions just to establish a pipeline. Although this didn't manifest, it did not prevent the CIA from continuing to try for in 1986 they drew up some more ideas to overthrow Syria by provoking sectarian tensions (does this sound familiar?). The same policy goals were desired again in 1991 and in 2001.

What we see now - with the supposed "civil war" in Syria – is that it has been years in the making and the recent efforts of ISIS and other terrorist extremist (all supported by the West and Saudi Arabia) may have finally come to fruition after hard work put in by the British government according to former French foreign minister Roland Dumas who is on record saying that he got it from the horse's mouth that "top British officials" were in the process of arming Sunni nationals "to invade Syria" in 2009 – two years before the anti-Assad protest. Then there is what then Secretary of State

Hillary Clinton said in 2012: that the best way to help Israel deal with Iranis to help overthrow Bashar Assad.

So it seems that President Trump is no different than Obama or Bush or his democratic opponent Hillary Clinton and their desire to use any excuse to make bankers and oil giants the benefactors of the wealth to be generated by a divided Syria without Assad at the helm. Chemical weapons like WMDs in Iraq, was contrived as an excuse to justify their goals. I mean we know that Turkey supplied Sarin gas to Syrian rebels in 2013 in order to frame the Syrian government. We also know that independent Humanitarian organizations have documented that ISIS has used chemical weapons, including Sarin, chlorine and sulfur mustard agents, at least 52 times on the battlefield in Syria and Iraq since 2014.

We also know that just like the Bush Administration, Hillary Clinton and Obama cooperated with Saudi Arabia's government to fund and arm clandestine operations designed to take down Iran and its ally Syria by encouraging Sunni extremist groups that not only champion a militant view of Islam but are also are anti-America and sympathetic to ISIS and Al Qaeda. All which seem to be from extremist Islamic fundamentalist groups with origins in or connections to Saudi Arabia.

In all sincerity, the west, as in Yemen, is backing the Muslim Brotherhood in Syria, Sunni's who are an openly admitted group that considers the U.S. and of Israel as lifelong enemies. By bombing Assad, we are basically s one writer put it serving as the ISIS/Al Qaeda Air force. This in my opinion, is no different that when Barack Obama invaded Libya without Congressional approval in 2011. Trump clearly is no different and seems to take his marching orders from the neoconservatives and neoliberals who won't be happy until a major U.S. military intervention happens in Syria (and other places) even if it means a confrontation with Russia and/or China. You may question my analysis but for what it is worth, NSC adviser Gen. H.R. McMaster is no dissimilar than Hillary Clinton, Victoria Nuland, or Nuland's husband – Robert Kagen on this matter.

Again as I asked in the beginning of this essay, is Trump any different than Bush or Obama? I suspect not. As one writer pointed out: "I don't think that anybody seriously believes that Assad or anybody else in the Syrian government really ordered a chemical weapons attack on anybody. To believe that it would require you to find the following sequence logical: first, Assad pretty much wins the war against Daesh which is in full retreat. Then, the US declares that overthrowing Assad is not a priority anymore (up to here this is all factual and true). Then, Assad decides to use weapons he does not have. He decides to bomb a location with no military value, but with lots of kids and cameras. Then, when the Russians demand a full investigation, the Americans strike as fast as they can before this idea gets any support. And now the Americans are probing a possible Russian role in this so-called attack. Frankly, if you believe any of that, you should immediately stop reading and go back to watching TV."

I remember the Gulf of Tonkin and other major U.S. lies to justify war like the one in 1970 when our government lied to the American people and said, "We didn't cross the border going into Cambodia" when in fact we did. Former UK ambassador to Syria, Peter Ford, was correct in his assessment equally when he said like Libya, Syria will "implode" if President Assad was removed from office period. Not to mention bombing Syria does nothing to provide humanitarian relief and merely distracts the world from the West supported atrocities in Yemen, Mosul and the South Sudan.

Ossoff, Carpetbaggers and Vacuum Cleaners

After the civil war in America, several new political terms were introduced into our lexicon, one of which was the word carpetbagger. A carpetbagger was a northerner who moved to the South during Reconstruction (1863–1877 or 1865-1870 depending who you read) mainly to seek political office in an area where they did not live. To be accurate, during Reconstruction most of the Republican governors in the South were from the North. This past week in Georgia, where I live and in a district, I don't, a carpetbagger managed to place himself in a run-off for the Georgia sixth congressional district and his name is Jon Ossoff. I will expound on this and in the process, introduce a new term of political etiquette, the "vacuum cleaner."

Ossoff like carpetbaggers back then were only concerned with self-interest that could be attained via exploitation. Exploitation in the sense that he is trying to profit by making use of and benefiting from resources from other cats outside of the 6th district to use the same district to enrich himself – nothing more or nothing less. Ask anyone in the 6th about him and you will quickly find out they don't know him or ever see him. He has raised millions of dollars from folk that ain't even in Georgia just to try and get the Republican seat in the special election vacated by Dr. Tom Price.

There are several reasons I consider Ossoff a carpetbagger throwback yet I will stick to two: that he doesn't live in the district he is running to represent and that he cannot even vote for himself in said district. I could add that I personally think Ragin Edwards, an actual East Cobb county and 6th district resident would have been the best choice for the Democratic party to support, but I should have known better based on the racist history of the Democratic party, that they would support a white man over a black woman who also happens to be a graduate of Georgia Tech. Then there is the fact that very little of his financial support comes from Georgians or folk that live in the 6th district. One source reported that he has raised tens of thousands from many of the Hollywood liberal and progressive elite, which proffers the question, what are they buying? Ossoff's campaign, per Politico had raised more than $8 million by the election date with more than 95 percent coming from out of state. The Atlanta Journal Constitution noted: "If 95 percent of Ossoff's $8.3 million was from out of state, that means 5 percent was from Georgians. And 5 percent of $8.3 million is $415,000."

I find it hard to consider that folk like Debra Messing, Rosie O'Donnell, Kyra Sedgwick, Chelsea Handler and actresses Jane Fonda know anything about the needs of Georgians to even comment or tell folk who to vote for. Not to mention that they most likely send their kids to private schools and have private security and therefore are unqualified to remark on such public issues on behalf of citizens involved in selecting their new representative. But who cares if out of state cats fund a Sixth District's Georgia candidate for the U.S. Congress who also doesn't live in the district they are running to represent and can't vote for himself in said district? True, Ossoff did get most the votes in the primary for the 6th district, but in terms of basic math, it was less than Republicans and independents combined.

But such logic is lost on the new political class of what I call "vacuum cleaners." I describe vacuum cleaners as a byproduct of this new social media age. They are hyperpartisan and typically are liberal progressive types that believe they are tolerant but are not. The suck up every and all bits of information that supports their political view and on places like twitter, RT their views which they get from other folk, all day long. A good sign that they are a vacuum cleaner is if most the folk they RT are from DC, New York, or California. You may see a Massachusetts, Chicago or Atlanta person RTd but not as much as an inside the beltway or NYC cat. Honestly, I think Democrats need to suck up this L because this past Tuesday they had their best chance in Georgia but the lost it.

Neoliberalism or How to Pimp
the Underclass in Six Syllables

For long as I can recall, at least after the civil rights era, the economic prosperity in the African American community has been on the decline. Ironically this started under the purview of a new approach to economics trumpeted to be the end all and be all to the problems (economic and civil) that confronted the U.S. since the end of the Vietnam war. This is what it was supposed to be but what it became was a new-fangled form of lassez-faire policy that to date, has serve to retard economic growth and increased disparities in wealth and income inequality in the U.S. and worldwide.

You got it, I am speaking about neoliberalism. I have defined neoliberalism policy as policy that transfers controls of economic factors from the public sector to the private sector. Neoliberals rather in the form of Ronald Reagan, Barack Obama, Tony Blair or The Clinton's assert that economic and foreign policy that removes trade barriers and restrictions on capital flows is the best thing you can do to create job growth, economic prosperity, wealth and more importantly, eliminate or at least, lift folk out of poverty. Although apolitical, after the 80s, democrats (social democrats in France, Labor in England and Democrats in the U.S.) used this ideology to usher in and promote their views on domestic and foreign policy. A strange occurrence, since historically, these political parties were framed as being the representative of the little man, main street, the factory worker and union member. Establishing neoliberal free market foreign and domestic would mean that the democrats would not have to work with the vulture class. This meant forming more relationships with the elite and wealth of the big cities more so than the lowly farmers of the Midwest or miners in other states. Even in urban areas, it meant economic ostracization for minority communities until it was time to secure their vote.

This alone demanded that Democrats listen and accept more ideas from the wealthy and affluent, and it has been the same since Tony Blair and the Clinton's. Although democrats proclaim their policies serve progressive and liberal objectives, the harsh reality is that the do not. They have led to the destruction of unions and reduction in collective bargaining rights while they claim to be the party of the working class. They have tightened relationships with the white-collar elite and for taking their money, have put in place policy that has help to suppress wages and wage growth. These policies have also resulted in the ruination of the auto industry as we have witnessed in Detroit. But they did not stop there. Starting with Bill Clinton, they even deregulated banks and had the gumption to tell the working poor that their situation was due to education, while rich liberals ignore the fact that even going to college, whether one finishes with a degree or not results in most African Americans having amassed nearly two times the amount of student loan debt than whites. Even Obama and other black establishment cats representing the democratic party got in on the act preaching the same credo asserting a culture of poverty argument that basically suggest that black are poor and need to go to college. As if all our problems are due more to having a poor education, than the neoliberal policies they unabatingly advance.

With Obama and his neoliberal economic locution, African American unemployment is still two times that of white unemployment. Economic disparity between whites and blacks has grown wider since his election and African American median income has fallen more than ten percent with twenty-six percent of Black households being considered "food insecure." Since Obama took office, the seasonally adjusted labor-force-participation rate for black Americans across the board has declined and the number of black food-stamp participants has increased more than fifty percent. Add to this that the percentage of black Americans who own homes has declined sharply and that real median income among black households based on data from your Census Bureau has also declined. This means a higher poverty rates for blacks since 2008, a reduction in the number of young black men with full-time employment and an increase in median white wealth providing them with more income at a pace way surpassing that of blacks under your administration. Maybe this is why it has been determined that single African American women ages 36 to 49 have a median wealth of $5. This is without me even mentioning the paltry rate of GDP growth since you took office. To put it bluntly, the economic liberalism of the Obama era was just a more murderous form of Reagan – unfettered (legal or illegal) immigration was encouraged and a blind eye was turn to both corporate tax evasion via overseas accounts and the activity of criminal banker activity on Wall Street.

All the can be connected in a causal manner to policy put in place by folk (99% democratic progressive liberals) elected to office or thought leaders, by the poor and working class black folk who have been distressed by said policies. Again, plainly put poverty and racism has only got worse during Obama's tenure. Obama and democrats love to tout a higher minimum wage as being a solution but never answer how is this possible, when even with a higher wage, you cannot be sure that cats will give folk the hours they need just to get by let alone move out of poverty? How can this solve any economic issues sustained for blacks since democrats came to power during the post-civil-rights era and with democrats still pushing for capitalist globalization that has had a disproportionately negative influence on African Americans over the past forty to fifty years? How can this help when 95% of the jobs created during the Obama Presidency were temporary? And don't say because we talk about education because the reality is that African Americans with some college education have higher unemployment rates than whites who never went to college or even completed high school?

It was President Obama in 2014 that stated "if Uncle Jethro would get off the couch and stop watching Sports Center and go register some folks and go to the polls, we might have a different kind of politics." This in a nut shell is neoliberalism, who's efficacy that even the IMF is starting to question. A philosophy which states we get rich if you vote for us and us alone while you black folk will remain restricted to unstable low wage service sector jobs (which are vanishing) and represent the fastest growing population of homeless in the U.S., women and children. This is one reason why economic position of African Americans have not changed since democrats began to represent all major urban areas since the mid-1960s. If I am wrong, then why have schools failed to improve and have been on a downward trend since then? Why have long-term job prospects in these same places decreased and even disappeared since then? Neoliberalism has never been shown to have been effective or even work in the real world, especially when it comes to improving the economic conditions of blacks regardless of location of residency. So, I ask you, why support a party that takes your vote and destroys your community and ability to enjoy life, liberty and the pursuit of happiness? Riddle me that Batman.

After Mosul, Will it be Erdogan or The Kurds?

This past week President Tayyip Erdogan had a meeting with President Trump. As observed before when he met with President Obama, once again his goons took to beating up and violently attacking protestors. But this is not important for the time being, what is pertains to the Trump administration plans for after the Mosul offensive and even ridding Syria of IS. This is valid for my main botheration with Obama was his failure to plan for what was to occur after the implementation of any of his foreign policy escapades from Yemen to Syria to the South Sudan and especially in Libya.

Unlike the prior administration, I can note that Trump seems to be engaged with the issues but I am not so certain that he grasps the seriousness of a fallout between Erdogan and Turkey and/or the US and the Kurds. Something must give and I am not at rest that President Trump, as Obama before him, is ready for this. And he is the one who opened this can of worms when his administration announced that the U.S. would back, arm and support the Kurds in their effort against the Islamic State and to show he was about that life, the Trump Defense Department immediately sent military vehicles with American flags to the YPG fighters engaged in combat activities on the Syrian side of the border.

As expected Erdogan was not happy and expressed such through one of his many mouth pieces this time being one of his top foreign policy advisers İlnur Çevik. Cevik expressed succinctly the differences between Washington and Ankara over the U.S. military's partnership with Kurdish military organizations in Syria by hinting that American troops could be targeted alongside their Kurdish allies in the country since U.S. forces have teamed up with members of the Kurdish People's Protection Units (YPG) and since Turkish fighter's patrol along the border region with Syria frequently bombing the YPG who they see more of an enemy than IS. Specifically, Cevik stated that if the U.S. troops would "go to far, our forces would not care if American armor is there, whether armored carriers are there" adding that "Suddenly, by accident, a few rockets can hit them."

It was a simple choice for Trump based on all he has been talking about wiping the Islamic State off the face of the planet. Easy also because the YPG have shown themselves to be one of the most effective forces on the ground in the fight against IS next to the Syrian Defense Forces. Moreover, most Kurds are Sunni Muslims, however, they consider themselves Kurds first, and Muslims second, and don't want to be absorbed into a universal caliphate or equally any affiliation with Sharia law. Also of importance is that the Kurds are the most pro-American people in the entire Middle East and believe and acknowledge equal right for women.

The fact is northern Syria has a large Kurdish population which for decades, Turkey has viewed a major political threat due to the mounting influence of the Kurdish Democratic Union Party (PYD) and the People's Protection Units (YPG) in the region. Erdogan was hoping the US-YPG alliance which President Barack Obama started would be discontinued under Trump. But it has not and he made this clear in an interview in which he stated that seeing US military vehicles operating close to the border with Syrian Kurdish fighters "seriously saddened" him.

The Kurdish and US soldiers who support them are during an offensive to take Raqqa, ISIS's Syrian capital, and have recently made significant gains against the extremists in the region but recent attacks by Turkey against Kurdish areas in Syria are hampering the offensive against ISIS. Erdogan doesn't want the YPG or the PYD to be the leading powers in Syria's Kurdistan region and sees both as part of the PKK.

To understand this one must understand the Kurds in the region (Iraq, Syria and Turkey). Erdogan's forces are fighting the Turkish Kurds (The PKK or Banned Kurdistan

Workers' Party led by Abdullah Ocalan who was jailed in 1999 with the help of U.S. CIA) and Erdogan is extremely hostile with the Syrian Kurds (the PYD or Democratic Unity Party) who are aligned with the PKK and have their own militia called the YPG. Last there are the Kurds in Iraq who have established a Kurdish Regional Government since the US invasion/occupation of Iraq and who have their own military forces called the Peshmerga. All three Kurdish areas are fighting IS, but all are considered problems to Erdogan. The Turks want to destroy the PKK and its affiliates, as well as the YPG. They consider them to be the same or equal to ISIS – terrorist. This is what the U.S. and Russia equally must syphon through because Erdogan sees the possible defeat of IS in Raqqa by the Kurds and U.S. forces as major political leverage for the YPG.

When the Turkish State was founded in the aftermath of WWI, the Kurds were promised the creation of an independent state as part of the treaty of Sevres in 1920. Unfortunately for them, this part of the treaty was never ratified and Turkey has refused to recognize the existence of a separate Kurdish ethnic community within its borders. Upon which several major Kurdish rebellions occurred in Kurdish strongholds in Turkey during the 1920s and 1930s. Since then the Turkish ruling class began viewing a separate Kurdish identity as a threat to the nation-state - Turkification.

Now Turkey has become one of the world's largest and most powerful Muslim fundamentalist states. I say this because it is well known that Erdogan's administration (maybe with the exceptions of the Saudi's) is the main state sponsor of ISIS. Add to this that Erdogan is an Islamist that embraces Muslim fundamentalism to the level of even destroying the last bits of democracy in Turkey to eradicate all Kurdish people so that he can establish a new Ottoman Empire for Turks and only Turks. Now, it is estimated that around fifteen million individuals of Kurdish origin live in

Turkey who under the present leadership of the Republic, have been treated worse than a second-class citizenry.

Trump and Putin know that they NEED the YPG to continue with its fight against the Islamic State. Although the U.S. has maintained good relations for the past seven decades, the war on ISIS has led the Pentagon to decide that it is the best interest of the U.S. to work with Kurdish forces if the objective is to defeat ISIS. Thus, the conflict: the U.S. want to work with the Kurds on the ground in Syria effort to take Raqqa (the headquarters of ISIS) but Turkey doesn't want this thinking that it with give them more clout with the current U.S. administration.

Like Obama (called Erdogan a trusted friend), Trump underestimates Erdogan's hatred of the Kurdish minority and the level of his support of ISIS. Trump must decide if its relationship with the Kurds in Syria is a temporary relationship of opportuneness until IS is defeated or is the beginning of something new? Something new that could lead to an independent Kurdistan? Erdogan wouldn't be happy about it, but he'd accept this from the U.S. and I believe that is his main concern. After all, we saw what he did after the strong electoral might of the Kurdish party that prevented a parliamentary majority of Erdogan's AKP in June's election.

America's Liberal Progressive Gleichschaltung

I have been paying attention to and observing a dangerous and growing trend of intolerance in the United States. Strange enough, it is coming from those that say they are the most tolerant of all people in America – progressive liberals. Even more odd-balled and even sickening, is that it is in my understanding of history, reminiscent one aspect of Nazification that was called Gleichschaltung. I say this for two reasons, first is that I speak and read German and second is that it played a vital role in Hitler's propaganda machine. By definition (if I could translate Gleichschaltung into English) the best I could come up with would be the "forcible coordination" of one to have the views and beliefs of the majority.

Over the years it has become popular and even acceptable for progressive democrats, when they do not agree with an opinion or perspective that is out of their narrative, to use force and coercion to try and get you to accept and see the world how they "want" you to see the world. In this ether of make-believe, dissenting voices, and frequently common sense, are not welcome. Consequently, the individual rights of American citizens inclusive of free speech are only for them and not you. This is the Gleichschaltung of National Socialism.

After the death of Paul von Hindenburg in 1934, Hitler took control of Germany with several goals in mind, one of which was to establish tight control over the nation. One way to accomplish this for him was to do all possible to guarantee that the National Socialist would be the most powerful party in Germany. He planned for the coordination of society by making all things an arm of the Nationalist Socialist party and referred to this as Gleichschaltung. This would enable him and the Nazi party to convert Germany into a totalitarian state. This was done by outlawing the expression of alternative views, beliefs and political perspectives and the use of propaganda to promote Nazi ideals.

Now if you read and think about this, no clearer explanation of what is happening around the U.S. from Berkeley to Harvard, to Yale and yes, even Evergreen College can be aptly describe as Gleichschaltung for the sake of having one single authoritative totalitarian view for all to follow. This would have never happened under Hitler without him gaining a strangle hold over cultural and educational beliefs. He could do it so effectively because he employed "Lansen' or a "language of the masses" that made it easier for the people to agree and accept the propaganda of Nazism.

This is what the progressive left is doing. In one breathe they say they are fighting against bias, intolerance, and hate-speech yet at the same time impose and employ hate-speech, intolerance and bias to communicate their messages which are often grounded in raw hate or a 'weaponized victimhood' directed at all that do not think as they do. It is a little comical yet telling of the state of the intellectual prowess of this incessantly offended generation. For example, they portend that they are tolerant because they are people who speak and/or act on beliefs that do not exclude entire groups of people, but ask for black only dormitories, black only graduations or order and require all white people to leave certain spaces even if they do not desire to do such. If people do exercise their first amendment rights, it's going to likely be some burning, window breaking, car destroying and all around chaos. Even worse, it seems as if they cannot even see how stupid their actions are for as I suggested prior, they have no interest or desire to participate in an open and honest discussion about anything (diversity, tolerance or inclusion) because like thee Nazi's, they are too superciliously self-righteous about the divinity and supremacy of their beliefs.

This is what the Gleichschaltung was designed to accomplished – using force to push ideals upon anyone through the threat of violence and Professor Bret Weinstein was correct to note that doing such was "an act of oppression in and of itself" because America's liberal progressive are doing the exact same thing. Why else would they back the hindrance of freedom of speech? What these students are doing is dangerous and to make matters worse, they have no idea of how bad what they are doing is, or either do not care. Moreover, they fail to recognize that they are neither progressive or liberal, but rather leftists for whom listening to a different point of view is impossible. They claim they are accepting of Muslims, blacks, women or members of the GLBTQ community, but that is only if they are progressive liberal democrats like themselves. Otherwise step off.

Yes, this is where we are in America, and for this participation trophy generation, if they do not win or get their way, they wear their soreloserness on their sleeves and cry and whine openly for all to see.

Give Me Flint and LA over Paris Any Day

I thought I couldn't see anything more ridiculous in the form of behaviors evinced by the progressive left since the election of Donald Trump. Personally, I thought I had seen it all, the entire range of everything running from pure vitriolic hatred and 'soreloserness' to overt and utter contempt and even fear of what his election appears to mean for them. But I was wrong.

This past week Trump kept a campaign pledge. On the stump, he said he would pull the U.S. out of the Paris Accords and as a man of his word, he did. Upon which, you would have thought that he fired every teacher in Baltimore or put up ten thousand confederate monuments or even poisoned the water of all the residents of Flint, Michigan and threatened them with foreclosure if they did not pay for water they could not bathe in or drink. I use these as examples because all of them are real and current events that should have the attention of all Americans regardless of political affiliation because they touch the very fabric of compassion and genuine concern for our fellow citizens. But no, this makes too much since so contrived outrage must suffice in the name of disagreement for disagreement sake.

There once was time when democrats looked out for the small man, but those days have been long gone. They ended with the rise of the corporatist liberal democrat – the

Bill and Hillary Clinton's (net worth= +$250 million), the Rep. John Delaney's (net worth = +$91.6 million), Nancy Pelosi's (net worth = +$29.3 million), the Mark Warner's (net worth = $90.8million), the Dianne Feinstein's (net worth = +$52.7), the Richard Blumenthal's (net worth = +$66.9 million) and yes, even the Obama's of the nation (net worth= +$24.5 million). So for this coterie of politician, it is not unusual for big global efforts to take precedence over local and national concerns. They speak loudly about Trump ending the Paris accord as known and signed by President Obama but seem to not be interested in the thousands of citizens of Flint still dealing with exorbitant levels of lead contamination in their tap water making it unsafe for them to drink or that homeowners are being told that if they do not pay for water unsafe to drink or use, the Democratic city government will put liens on their properties. If they are unable to pay, they may lose their homes. This isn't as outrageous as Paris.

Therefore, I cannot comprehend why withdrawing from the Paris Accord is such a lightning rod. Not that it impacts anyone personally, just for the mere fact Donald Trump did it and that it was undoing what their favorite politician of all time – President Obama had put in place. This is typical of the cognitive dissonance the left has been displaying since last November. For example, Democratic Mayor Catherine Pugh of Baltimore has stated that she's considering removing Confederate statues from the city following what the democratic leadership in New Orleans just did. Not because her citizens and electorate asked her, but because she thinks it is cool. Albeit it will be at a cost of about $200,000 a statute to tear them down. This is not the point of confusion. Although this seems to have the Mayor's attention, school officials just informed 115 Baltimore City staff members that they will be laid off in the next few weeks. These include school guidance counselors, librarians, assistant principals and classroom teachers. The Baltimore City Public School system presently has a $130 million budget gap to fill. Ironic isn't it, Baltimore can find money to take down statues and send them down a memory hole but can't find the loot to keep needed educators in a school system that is one of the poorest performing school districts in the nation and serves some of the poorest children in the USA.

I expected that former Obama Administration cats would vehemently hate on Trump's decision which was clear from tweets by the likes of Dan Pfeiffer, Susan Rice and Cody Keenan. I also anticipated that trick azz world leaders would also complain, also as evidenced by the tweets of Nicola Sturgeon, Prime Minister of Denmark Lars Rasmussen, former Mexican president Vincente Fox and others. What surprised me was seeing every black negro progressive liberal democrat this side of the moon express a similar emotionally uninformed deportment. Now nothing wrong with that, but the reality is that 99% of both groups (politicians and black folk in America, ain't never even read the Paris Agreement. Honestly, I haven't read the entire agreement, but rather just the UN background document on the agreement. So, I don't know what is exactly in it and as such will not address it.

This is another reason I find this fervid outrage comical, cats aligning with the Paris Agreement and don't know what the fck the accord is even about. What I do know is that America must dole out a large chunk of chump change to get this Paris party started and where there is free loot, the people will not benefit but you can best believe big corporate interests are looking to get their slimy paws on the billions in incentives and subsidies guaranteed in the accord to develop green energy sources. In my opinion, we could use that money elsewhere. For example, over the past year, the homeless population in Los Angeles County is twenty-three percent than it was in 2016. More worrisome is that the Los Angeles Homeless Services Authority reported a sixty-one percent increase in homeless youth compared to 2016. This even though the Democratic leadership of the city promised to spend $138 million on homelessness this year (which thus far has proven to me a windfall for big real estate).

Again, these are the people loudly upset and pained with Trump for removing the U.S. from the Paris Accord. Yet they are cool with a growing homeless population in their midst and seem to never have money for black people in jails who need access to public defenders but can find money out of nowhere to fund a plus $10 million legal defense fund for illegal criminal immigrants facing deportation.

So, call me what you will, I have no problem with, nor see anything wrong with Trump pulling out of the Paris Accord. So, we won't be giving millions too oil rich nations to help them at the expense of other poor nations. The way I see it, Fck Paris, give me Flint, Baltimore, Los Angeles or any other American city any day. I guess my comportment is unacceptable for the Liberal Progressives – actually putting American's first.

The Snap, Crackle & Pop of Susan Rice

Now I don't watch the Sunday network talk shows, but I do get to read the transcripts. I was sent one via email from a friend of mine on Susan Rice's appearance on the Sunday talk show hosted by Former Bill Clinton Press Secretary George Stephanopoulos. My friend was cracking up and couldn't stop laughing. Now for the record I like Susan Rice, I may not agree with her often, but I do like her (nothing like a smart black woman to make me smile). I digress. Nonetheless, it was obvious the powers that be on the mainstream media wanted or needed to get former Ambassador Susan Rice into the collective unconscious of the public left.

From reading the transcript, the first thing that jumped out was that Stephanopoulos was tossing former Ambassador Rice under hand softball pitches or even worse, setting the ball on the T for her to hit without much difficulty. The set up (as has been the case since the presidential primary), is to first use a few of Trump tweets like they were chum (fish parts, bone and blood) to attract the anger and lure Ambassador Rice like a shark to the Trump smell. This is followed by the introduction of the Great White or Tiger Shark they are baiting (chumming) for: this time it being the person who served as national security adviser and UN ambassador under President Obama. His first question, referring to the commixture of tweets pertained to how alarmed should we be because of the recent terrorist attacks in London? Rice gave the basic scripted Benghazi type answer: "We need to remain very focused on dealing with that threat. But at the same time, we need to recognize that there will be homegrown extremists in all our countries. And there is no easy way to predict and defeat every single one of them."

Stephanopoulos's next question was pure chum. "You heard the president say that travel ban would bring an extra level of safety. Your response?"

RICE: "Well, George, there's really no evidence to suggest that by banning Muslims or banning Muslims from a particular set of six countries that we would make ours here in the United States safer. And that's, I believe, one of the major reasons why the courts thus far have been very skeptical of the travel ban. Moreover, I think there's a very real risk that by stigmatizing and isolating Muslims from particular countries and Muslims in general that we alienate the very communities here in the United States whose cooperation we most need to detect and prevent these homegrown extremists from being able to carry out the attacks."

Yes, that is correct, targeting the same predominantly Muslim nations Obama did in 2011 would only result in the "real risk that by stigmatizing and isolating Muslims from particular countries and Muslims in general that we alienate the very communities here in the United States." It would be easy to conclude then that Obama's slowing down of refugees and the level of Iraqi resettlement, would have resulted in the same. Now both programs are different, but it is the logic (or illogic) that sticks out as peculiar.

His next line of questioning briefly (and I mean briefly) addressed leaks. From reading the transcript and lack of follow-up by Stephanopoulos it was clear he did not want to accidently ask her about possible leaks and unmasking by Obama administration appointees so he deftly moved to the next subject which was her critique of President Trump published in *The New York Times*. Stephanopoulos stated, "… one of the things you wrote is that Russia has been a big winner under President Trump. How so?"

RICE: "Well, George, the United States has been the leader of the world because the world trusts and respects us, because we have an unprecedented network of alliances with close partners that work with us, whether it's to defeat ISIS, whether it's to deal with a threat of an Iranian nuclear weapon, or to go after challenges of a new sort like pandemic disease or climate change. We need these partners. And when we alienate our western allies, when the president went to NATO and failed to reaffirm, as every president has since 1948, that we're committed and remain committed to the defense of our NATO partners, he sent shockwaves through Europe. And that is exactly what Vladimir Putin wants. Because Putin's interests, as he reaffirmed just on Friday, is to see NATO weakened and ultimately destroyed. And when the United States, the most important player in NATO, casts doubt about our commitment to that vital alliance, it undermines our security. It undermines the security of our closest allies. And it's a big win for Vladimir Putin."

Now what is missing from this response you might ask? For starters, it is questionable if the prior administration tried to or wanted to go after ISIS. Obama did call them the JV team and blamed everyone in the universe (Bush, the second amendment & even global warming) for his not recognizing them as a threat. In fact, Obama was occupied with Al-Qaeda and Osama bin Laden so much so that he basically breast fed ISIS into existence with his policy of unilateral invasion of Libya under the dress of NATO. Which reminds us of how poorly he and Rice responded to the death of Ambassador Chris Stevens. Moreover, the concept that Iran as a major nuclear threat is also laughable given that they are still on the path and the deal negotiated by team Obama does nothing to prevent them from becoming a nuclear power. Not to mention the illegal and off the record $1.7 billion payment to Iran in 2016 made entirely in cash, with non-U.S. currency.

When asked about President Putin, Rice quickly responded that "he's lying" and that "The reality is, …the Russian government, at the highest levels, was behind the very unprecedented effort to meddle in our 2016 presidential election." Continuing she said, "Russia is an adversary. Russia not only has invaded a sovereign country and annexed part of it in Ukraine and Crimea (after Obama orchestrated coup). It's not only in cahoots with a regime in Syria that uses chemical weapons (yet to be proven), it has interfered directly and deliberately at the direction of the highest levels of its government in our democratic process…That is a threat to the integrity of our democracy. That's a threat to our country on a bipartisan basis. And we need to hold Russia accountable."

Who else to know if someone is lying than the always honest Susan Rice who had the gumption to go on national television and lie to hundreds of millions of U.S. citizens and people around the globe when on one news show she said: "Based on the best information we have to date, what our assessment is at present is in fact what began spontaneously in Benghazi as a reaction to what had transpired some hours earlier in Cairo where, of course, as you know, there was a violent protest outside of our embassy, sparked by this hateful video….We do not — we do not have information at present that leads us to conclude that this was premeditated or preplanned. I think it's clear that there were extremist elements that joined in and escalated the violence. Whether they were al-Qaeda affiliates, whether they were Libyan-based extremists or al-Qaeda itself I think is one of the things we'll have to determine."

Again Stephanopoulos let her hit the pitch right up the middle of the field without making a play on the ball. Without a transition, it was easy for him too move to the next point of liberal discontent – when he asked, "Would it have been appropriate for Jared Kushner to have a back-channel during the transition? Your successor, General McMaster, has suggested there's nothing wrong with it."

RICE: "Well, George, I think, these reports, if accurate, are concerning, not just because of communication between the Trump transition and the Russian government, and we do have communications between transition teams and foreign governments, but rarely with adversaries like the Russians, and rarely with the frequency that we have seen. But what I found most concerning about that report, which, if true, is that Jared Kushner suggested to the Russian ambassador that they communicate using Russian communications in a Russian diplomatic facility to hide their conversation from the United States government. That's extraordinary, if not mind-boggling from the point of view of a national security professional. I have worked in this field for 25 years. And I have never heard of such a thing. The United States -- and from one administration to the next -- has one government, one president at a time. And we worked very hard to do a professional and effective handoff. A seamless one. We worked very hard in this transition to accomplish that and to do so transparently."

This was probably the most historically inaccurate and artfully mendacious crock of Buffalo feces of the entire interview. First communication alone is not as heinous as Rice makes it out to regardless of who is President or what country it is, even Russia. And the part about advisories is either the result of a historically ill-informed person or a calculated lie.

After the election of Richard Nixon in 1968, his future national security adviser Henry Kissinger set up a backchannel to contact and communicate with the Soviet leadership via a known KGB operative named Boris Sedov, whom Kissinger had come to know from interactions at Harvard. Even before Nixon, FDR's used a long time fried Harry Hopkins as a go between the U.S., U.K. and Stalin. Only difference was that Roosevelt was President at the time. Then there's Obama's backchannel fiasco with Iran which occurred in 2008 while he was running for president in which prior to even being elected, his staff established secret communications with the Iranian leadership using William Miller to relay how they planned to interact with Iran if Obama was elected.

I don't know if Rice believes what she says in interviews or rather if she just like hearing herself talk. One thing for certain is that she has a short memory span and her knowledge of history is suspect or intentionally confined. I mean, the Obama administration and the democrats went from loving Russia to hating Russia and calling the nation the greatest threat in the world when just a little while back it wasn't.

Qatar: Is it about Trump, Israel or Nascent Influence?

Now as most of my readers know, I voted for Donald Trump, as well as I voted for Barack Obama in 2008. This is one reason I do not see a difference between democrats and republicans. Moreover, my voting for whomever doesn't come with me supporting them just because they received my vote. Rather, it requires I speak up objectively about policy and events that occur under their leadership that in my view I consider to be wrong-headed and generally fcked up. The recent severing of all relations with Qatar by Saudi Arabia, Bahrain, Egypt and the United Arab Emirates coincidentally after a visit from President Donald Trump in my opinion is such an event. Supposedly or at least based on media reports, because Qatar has relationships with the Muslim Brotherhood and Hamas and funds terrorism in the region. Iraq has indicated that they will not be taking sides on this issue.

Saudi Arabia has demanded that Qatar ends these relationships and this has left me scratching my head. Did Trump give a green light for this, knowingly or unknowingly? How far will this go? How will this impact any of the recent OPEC agreements? What could or would the worst-case scenario be? Why now? The fear of other area nations, namely Oman and Kuwait is that tensions may escalate and result in more unforeseen problems for all Gulf Cooperation Council (GCC) member states, maybe even a possible break-up of the GCC.

So far the Saudi royal family has imposed a naval blockade stopping most if not all of its maritime trade and more importantly Qatar's ability to export Liquefied natural gas is natural gas and oil. They have also closed their borders with Qatar, which immediately led to a run-on food the Qatari capital of Doha and suspended the license of Qatar Airways and ordered its banks to sell tall Qatari currency. The Saudi's have also ordered their citizens out of Qatar and gave

Qataris abroad 14 days to return to Qatar. Now Saudi Arabia has given Qatar 24 hours to fulfill 10 conditions given to Kuwait's emir, Sheikh Sabah Al Ahmad Al Jaber Al Sabah, who is operating as a mediator between Saudi and Qatar. If Qatar does not conform to the Saudi's request, will a military operation be on the table for Riyadh?

President Recep Erdogan of Turkey has come out in support of Qatar and questions the validity of the Saudi's allegations and their effort to isolate Doha. But this isn't too much of an unexpected position for Erdogan to take, since the ruling AKP party is a Muslim Brotherhood affiliate and both have provided support for the Muslim Brotherhood in Egypt and groups currently fighting to overthrow Syrian President Bashar al-Assad. Erdogan has also decided to deploy troops to Qatar after the 24-hour Saudi ultimatum was made. As part of an agreement signed in 2014 Turkey set up a military base in Qatar like the US base in Qatar. In his most recent statement about the growing tensions, Erdogan noted he did not consider sanctions against Qatar as being a good idea and added that in his view, the other nations were trying to impose a "guardianship over Qatar, which is in itself a violation of its sovereignty, and is rejected outright."

Honestly it is a weak argument for the Saudi's and their supporting cast and Trump needs to seriously monitor and evaluate this situation. Saudi Arabia calling another nation out for funding terrorism is like the pot calling the kettle black. Although Saudi Arabia has provided no proof to support its claims against Qatar, the history books do confirm that the Saudi's have remained as being one of the biggest sources of funding to so-called jihadi groups going back decades. Notwithstanding that nine of the fifteen 911 terrorist were from Saudi Arabia. So, there must be something else behind this.

Maybe it is Israel. We all know they have been trying for decades to drive a wedge between the Arab states. True,

Israel has worked with Doha and maintains amenable relationships but they have also let it be known of how their authentic feelings about the small nation. Israel may see this as an opportunity to drive a wedge between the Arab states (if the words of defense minister Avigdor Lieberman reflect the position of the Netanyahu administration and their views of all the Sunni Arab countries except for Qatar) who do not see a nuclear Iran as the number one threat in the middle east).

We know there has been bad blood between the Saudi's and Qatar for decades most likely starting with overthrow of the former Emir of Qatar, Sheikh Khalifa bin Hamad al-Thani by his son. Plus, there are a few other events over the past 20 years have seem to support this position. If I were asked, I'd say this was about the future of the middle east and energy resources. Doha doesn't agree with the Saudi view of how the middle east should be. In fact, they have openly shown how the despise the tyrants and dictators in the region including Saudi, Egypt and the Emirates and Qatar is on record for being willing to negotiate with Iran. The Saudi clique on the other hand see a single direction for the middle east which could shape it for many years to come. They are against and move toward democratic rule which is one reason they hate the Muslim Brotherhood and Hamas (which regardless of being terrorist or not, push for bottom up government). This is something the monarch's fear and a reason why some suggest Saudi pushed for Present Egyptian President El-Sisi to take over Egypt. The Saudi's have also given the world Salafism and Wahhabism and have been funding every Islamic fundamentalist ultra-conservative movement in support of jihad since the beginning of OPEC. Without the Saudi's we would have never had Osama bin Laden or Abu Bakr al-Baghdadi.

Sisi served as Egypt's military attaché in Riyadh before returning to Egypt. Evidence supports that he was and remains paid and supported by the Saudi government, who used him to overthrow the democratically elected leader of Egypt Mohamed Morsi (again, they fear popular democratic rule and to stop such in Egypt, the had to overthrow the leader the people elected). One could say that it is the desire for the Saudi's to stop all and every democratic movement in the region and maintain their feudalistic political domination, even if that means war as is evident for their support for bombing even other Sunni nations like Yemen and Syria. Qatar was very critical of Sisi killing thousands of civilians during his Coup while Saudi Arabia, Egypt and the Emirates were silent. Qatar is also anti secularist, dictatorships and unaccountable royals pushing their weight around and they express this openly.

This is about punishing Qatar not terrorism, so what is going on and why now? Qatar is a major energy producer and has become the single biggest natural gas supplier in the region. The offshore North Field, the world's largest liquid natural gas reservoir which they share with Iran, may also be a causal factor for Saudi Arabia's new stance. This may be why the Saudi's acted so abruptly (it can no longer be a stepchild of Saudi Arabia based on its increasing financial influence alone). Then there is the little item of Qatar removing a self-imposed ban on working with Iran to work jointly in operating the North Field. This not only angers the Saudi's but Israel equally, and only worsen the fact that the government in Doha has refused to sign on to the Saudi-Israel alliance (against Iran).

If the Trump team is smart, they may be able to take advantage of the good relationship the US military has with Qatar to squash this nonsense. As it stands, no one knows were Trump stands other than a few tweets which in my observation are just pouring gasoline on an already burning part of the globe. First Trump applauded the actions against Qatar, but later stressed the need for unity by the GCC during a phone call with Saudi King Salman. Moreover, Qatar is the location of al-Udeid air base, the U.S. largest airfield in the region were all missions for Syria are originated.

So, I don't have the answers, but it interesting to think about and I would rather occupy my mind with this than nonsensical Russia Trump collusion BS. I feel that Qatar will be alright and that nations including but not limited to Iran, Russia, China, and Turkey will jump to fill the void. I also see this as a fight among two versions of extreme Islam and as the Saudi's overtly showing their fear for a Shia dominated middle east. I worry about Saudi military intervention in Qatar but do not fear of any Saudi annexation and occupation of Qatar: Qatar shares largest natural gas field in the world with Iran, and they won't allow an occupation or invasion to happen.

Helmut Kohl's Death Reminds us of NATO's Uselessness

A while back around September, I started to write about why I agreed with those individuals that considered, or expressed the view that the North Atlantic Treaty Organization was obsolete. However, I refrained after reading other people expressing a historical viewpoint that was similar to mine and I did not want to just throw up more words on the same topic just in a different sequence and syntax of word usage. But I have decided to revisit this topic upon the passing of former Chancellor of Germany Helmut Kohl.

If we walk back in time to 1989, right before the fall of the Berlin wall, we would be able to see that the issues that concerned the western political establishment regarding German re-unification are similar in structure and content to those made in contradiction of the utility of NATO some 30 years later. What is going to happen to the stability of Europe that has been maintained ever since the end of the cold-war? Could and will Gorbachev (easily synonymous with Putin) accept the end of East Germany (soviet tanks were there at the time)? What will happen to the Eastern borders of Europe (especially Poland in 1989 ironically where NATO is conducting war games currently)?

As then, these issues and questions persist and frequently brought up by pro-Hillary Clinton progressive Neoliberal NATO-crats and folks like Sen. John McCain who recurrently speaks out openly to convict any effort to normalization US and EU relations with Russia (Putin). This is done any time they get, like a talentless rapper who hypes the real star on stage, they hype-up the fake news that presents Russia being a military threat in Eastern Europe (and anywhere else if the can - see Syria). Seems some NATO or Brussel's big wheel (Secretary-General Jens Stoltenber & German DM Ursulla von der Leyen) comes out of the back room every day to try and show how much they hate Russia over the next man or woman also.

Once upon a time NATO was simply a treaty designed to keep an occupying US army on European soil. Now it is just an outdated means of increasing US influence more so than being able to provide any real security anywhere. Basically, it is just a cash cow that seeks ways to justify immense military spending over the delusion America and European hallucination that we are perpetually on the brink of war with Russia, as well as a repurposed weapon of global neocolonialism and the tool of choice for regime change and national building. Thus, it's clear that many have a serious interest in seeing the status quo (NATO) continue.

Dr. Kohl's death is a reminder of this and that diplomacy is a skill set that is mandatory if peace and not war is truly the desired outcome for all conflicts. We must recall that the French said Kohl's plan for German reunification was out of the question and there was a lot of resistance to the idea of a united Germany in general. Most (France and the UK) felt it would change the balance of the EU forever and it did. Not to mention there was the old axiom - NATO was designed to keep the Russians out, the US military machine in Europe and the Germans down. Making one Germany destroyed all three of these prospects. Moreover, Kohl's success destroyed the justification for the incessant funding of the NATO war machine.

Probably the best detailed account of what Dr. Kohl had to deal with is described in *Mitterrand, the End of the Cold War, and German Unification* by Frédéric Bozo. Bozo describes how it only took Kohl less than a month to preempt all concerns from France, the U.K. and the United States when he came up with a 10-point plan to fast-track German unification. Of all his actions, his pledge to recognize the post-war German-Polish border (Oder-Neisse line) and his promise to pay for the cost of the Soviet troop withdrawal from East Germany were both shrewd and savvy and led to the end of the cold war. One could also posit that the post-Cold War reconfiguration of NATO that occurred after Kohl's unification of Germany was the start of the post WWII uselessness of NATO.

The fall of the Berlin wall was then followed by Gorbachev dissolving the Warsaw Pact and relinquishing control over all the Soviet-occupied Eastern European countries. This should have been the end of NATO since it was formed and established to serve as a cooperative security peacetime military alliance against the Soviet Union and Warsaw Pact Nations. Kohl's efforts also included getting the U.S. to promise that we would never expand NATO further eastward if he didn't object to East Germany's becoming a member of NATO.

Given the history, hard not to disagree but Donald Trump or anyone else as it regards NATO usefulness. Fact is that when the Berlin Wall fell, and the Soviet Union dissolved, the reason for the formation and maintenance of NATO ended too. If you want to keep it real, NATO was never capable of defending Europe without the US and its mission still hasn't evolved to keep up with threat of international terrorism and combatting the Islamic State. Problem is when you openly say such, you end up hurting the feelings of the D.C. neoliberal establishment war machine profiteer cartel. Cats the likes of Will Marshall, Richard Perle, Paul Wolfowitz, Robert Kagan, and Stephen Hadley who see NATO to extend their crony capitalistic ways. These are the folk who are the maddest when Trump and others point out that NATO freeloader nations need to "pay up or get out."

Yes, Kohl reminds me of how archaic and old-fashined and unserviceable NATO is. Nations like Albania, Croatia Poland, Hungary, Bulgaria, Estonia, Latvia, Lithuania, Romania, Slovakia, and Slovenia are all member states now (although the U.S. promised Gorbachev that NATO would not encroach upon Russia's borders). It is easy to see that in 2017 it has a single purpose: to serve as bait to start a world war with Russia.

Instead of heeding the wisdom of former statesmen before Kohl like Sen. Robert A. Taft in 1949 or President Eisenhower's via his prophetic cautioning in 1961 that "we must guard against the acquisition of unwarranted influence, whether sought or unsought, by the military-industrial complex," the west has yet to objectively examine the utility of NATO – especially if the desire is peaceful co-existence globally. Taft understood all of this and saw the formation of NATO, regardless of what was said, as "an offensive and defensive military alliance against Russia," saying that he believed "such an alliance is more likely to produce war than peace. A third world war would be the greatest tragedy the world has ever suffered." True, the UN Charter supposedly only allows nations to use force only in self-defense when under threat of imminent attack, but it seems that NATO knowing it is no longer valid, is just itching to provoke a fight with Putin, against reason and even to the detriment of humanity.

From Ernie Pyle to CNN

I grew up in the 1960s and although there was inherent bias evinced in the press during that time in both print and television media particularly regarding race, there remained objectivity when it came to covering basic news events and stories. This was a time in which I can still remember the folks I read in the local newspapers in my hometown in Memphis and occasionally when I would read the *Tennessean* out of Nashville, *Chicago Tribune* or *New York Times* at the library. But mostly it was the *Commercial Appeal*, the *Memphis Press-Scimitar* and the *Tri-State Defender*. I can even still recall reading the writings of Seymour Hersh, Rheta Grimsley Johnson and Ted Knap as well as watching the evening news reports by Walter Cronkite, David Brinkley and Ed Bradley - although there were only four TV channels then.

Unfortunately, all good things come to an end and what I was raised to consider journalism and objective reporting to service the need of the people and republic first has molded into the sinew of vile partisan collectivism practiced to serve and maintain a plutocratic status quo – something unheard of in the times of award winning journalist Ernie Pyle.

Now I am not as too well-versed on Pile as many maybe and first became acquainted with him as a child when I was collecting stamps (which I still do). It was beautiful brown and white 16 cent stamp that came out in 1971. I remember my mother bringing me home a block of four freshly minted stamps which I still have this day. Next I began to find out more about him. The only book I found at my neighborhood library was a collection of his newspaper columns from World War II titled *Brave Men*.

Just revisiting it now, makes me wonder what would so called journalist of this incessant 24 hour a day cable news generation think of Pyle's work and skill and most importantly, his objectivity. One would never imagine or even picture a 21st century war reporter joining in battle with a platoon they were covering and embedded with during a firefight on the battlefield. Yet this is our reality – we have gone from Ernest Taylor Pyle to CNN and a bevy of leftist and selfish misfits parading as journalist with names like Bash, Acosta, Blitzer, Cooper, Cuomo, Tapper and Lemon. To be honest, I can say the same for other similar news outlets too numerous to name (The Guardian, MIC, MSNBC, Huffington Post, Bloomberg, New York Magazine, New York Times, Vanity Fair & Vox), however, CNN has managed to put themselves out in front of even the nearest competitors for lack of honest reporting, objectivity and being truthful about their ulterior motives – which if I may state in my opinion is to bias and slander all things Trump and prop up the democratic party by any means required (see Kathy Griffin). Then there is the recent real-life example that resulted in three of their news staff being forced to resign over what seems to be a continuous trail of contrived stories on Russia/Trump collusion based on a single anonymous source, which had to beretracted.

This was not the first time. Earlier this month right before CNN hyped-up former FBI Director James Comey's opening testimony in front of the Senate Intelligence Committee, Gloria Borger, Jake Tapper and several others published a story (based on anonymous sources) that Comey was expected to dispute President Trump's claims that he had been told on multiple occasions by then Director Comey he was not under investigation. To make a short story shorter, they issued a retraction (they were wrong).

From Trump threatening to invade Mexico and the made-up removal of MLK's bust from the Oval office to the fabricated increase in suicide deaths of transgenders since his election to the fake Treasury Secretary SteveMnuchin foreclosing on an elderly woman over some pocket change story, the Ernie Pyle's and Ed Bradley's are few and between them are thousands of hack's named Josh Rogin, Anne Applebaum, Dana Schwartz, Sarah Silverman, Keith Olbermann, Matthew Yglesias, Reza Aslan and Joy Ann Reid.

We may have to accept that what was once consider journalism has been thrown out of the window for ratings and partisan demagoguery. Whether it is intentionally distorting the record or exact quotes to make a point as was in the case of Betsy DeVos (*Slate & The Daily Beast*) or fake news by omission as in the recent example of NBC's Meet The Press Host Chuck Todd interviewing Vermont Sen. Bernie Sanders about the Republican health care bill but nothing about Sanders and his wife being under FBI investigation in relation to bank fraud. I am almost certain if it were trump or any of his associates this would have led the questioning and there would have likely been no mention of the health care bill.

I hope we do not have to settle for the above as being reflective of the new standards of journalism. But it may just be that in the future, we should expect CNN political correspondents and Democratic operative to be synonymous and expect them to give questions to their hand-picked political favorites as standard operating procedure in the future. Maybe this is where we have landed in this brave new world, in a place where intellectual dishonesty is preferred to accuracy and smearing individuals you do not agree with is paramount than honest and objective coverage for the well-being of the country and public good, even if it means making up fabricated single unnamed sources stories that are unverified about Russia collusion with the executive branch and contrived election interference. Personally, I have not had cable or television on my farm since 2006. I say cut off the idiot box but also recognize that such is difficult for individuals not mentally tough enough to move away from the group think of the heard. We have truly come a long way from Ernie Pyle.

The Awkward Electoral Dance of Liberal Democrats

When I look at the current state of U.S. liberal democrats, it reminds of watching a semi-cool white person on the streets of Memphis trying to juk. They are more than out of place, off rhythm and seemingly unaware of both, which puts them out of touch with reality and the perspectives of others watching them. It is as if they did not learn any lessons from the victory of Donald Trump in 2016 and like zombies, respond to only things that they see the mainstream media tell them to be outraged about. No real issues, just outrage here, outrage there, here an outrage, there an outrage, everywhere an outrage. Russia collusion or Russian hacking. Trump tweeted this or Trump tweeted that. It is like the dance of the person in Memphis, awkward and an indicator of the dim electoral future liberals have in the U.S. if they do not get on beat.

For starters, they saw what worked for Trump and Bernie Sanders yet they pull out the same old veer offense that continues to turn the ball over after three downs. They should be able to observe that they need a similar and HONEST message presented by a younger and more genuine person, not just some east or west coast big wig city elite to garble mumbo jumbo on thirty second commercials that don't offer policy solutions for everybody. Instead they run out city slick carpetbagger named Ossoff to run in a district in which he did not live in and spend $2 3million and worse, did not harvest as many votes as Rodney Stooksbury, the Democrat listed on the ballot during the general election last November. Or as Newsweek put it: "Rodney Stooksbury, who raised no money and had no campaign website or online presence."

Trump can say the word puzzy and liberals run out of their house to protest, complain and destroy property, yet seem to forget and equally said nothing and saw no offence in President Obama bombing kids around the globe and cats in Flint have no water to drink and being ordered by democrats to pay for what they cannot consume or face foreclosure. Rep. Sheila Jackson Lee just recently called for President Trump to resign for his tweets attacking Mika Brzezinski. Last I heard the dozens isn't illegal. Putting it plainly it is like Mika saying "Donald you dumb and ride the retarded bus" and Trump responding "yo momma smoke crack rock." End of story (if you cannot stand the heat get out of the kitchen).

This is just one problem; how do they justify calling themselves liberal or progressive if they ignore global suffering and continue to promulgate neoliberal policy that causes suffering not only in the US but around the globe because of wars promoting the global imperialistic goals of neoliberal republicans and democrats?

This dance doesn't end there. As 2018 quickly approaches, they still lack not only a solid policy message but also candidates. They have Tulsi Gabbard who is on the record calling for restoring Glass-Steagall, consistently is opposed to regime change, is against any cuts to Medicare or Social Security and the NSA's bulk collection of data. But Gabbard speaks her mind and equally goes against the core liberals in the democratic party. This faction question her passion for LGBT and abortion rights. They also will never forget that she doesn't tote the party line on fundamental Islamic terrorism noting that for over the last decade most terrorist attacks conducted around the world are the result of "radical Islamic ideology." Even more of a concern for the democratic establishment was her resolution she introduced to prioritize Christians and Yezidis — when granting refugee status.

But Gabbard is ignored and even avoided, just as several other noteworthy leaders of the new school like Kimberly Ellis (as the vote for the Democratic party chair of California held its election demonstrated) and former Ohio state senator Nina Turner. Instead they prefer others like New Jersey senator Cory Booker, Maryland congressman John Delaney and relative newcomer Senator Kamala Harris of California.

Harris is interesting, she has come to political fruition after she was cut off by her colleagues in the Senate while she questioned Attorney General Jeff Sessions (an event that she quickly used to raise tens of thousands of dollars) and came to politics being the 29-year-old girlfriend of California Assembly Speaker Willie Brown when he was 60. In 1994 Brown named Harris to the California Medical Assistance Commission, before that he appointed her to the state Unemployment Insurance Appeals Board. She was described by several people at the Capitol as Brown's girlfriend." Harris barley was elected California's Attorney General in 2010 by about 50,000 after provisional ballots were counted. While AG, her department argued against expanding the early release program for inmates on the basis that it would deplete the cheap (slave) labor force. Many see Harris as a corporatist and in the mold of the establishment democratic core of the state.

These inconsistencies make the democrats seem fickle. Take the recent health care debate ironically, in California. Nurses, unions and average citizens were overwhelming in support of what was described as a single payer Medicare for all (the Healthy California Act). But Democrats who maintain complete control of the state to pass a bill like this, did the opposite. In support of corporate donors in the healthcare, insurance and pharmaceutical industries, Democratic state Assembly Speaker Anthony Rendon helped to block a Democrat-sponsored bill to create the Healthy California Act. Reports indicate that Rendon has taken in more than $101,000 from pharmaceutical companies and another $50,000 from major health insurers over the past 5 years. This is par for the course considering that the California Democratic Party has received more than $1.2 million from the specific groups opposing the bill, and more than $2 million from pharmaceutical and health insurance industry donors.

Democrats must show that they are the party of the people. However, their addiction to corporate plutocratic funding seems to prevent them from being able to do such. Not to mention that it abrogates the voices of the citizenry they claim to represent. The liberal establishment wing of the Democratic party is cleary out of touch, out of step and off beat – awkward choreography sure to lead them to where they do not want to be in 2018.

Why Black Folks Need Confederate Monuments

Some may or may not know that one of my favorite books of all time is *1984* written by George Orwell. To be honest, since about ten years of age, I've must have read this book more than 20 times. Each time I read it I come away with something new. To refresh your memory, the main character in the book is a man named Winston Smith. Smith works in the Records Department in the Ministry of Truth, where his job is to rewrite history per the desires of the Party that runs the totalitarian government of Oceania. Specifically, he revises old writings, politically inconvenient facts and history to advance the propaganda interests of the Oceania government. One tool Orwell invents for this purpose was the memory hole.

In *1984*, Orwell describes a memory hole as an opening in a wall connected to a tube that is connected to an incinerator. It is employed to destroy any inconvenient or embarrassing fact on historical records that is no longer considered useful for politics. In addition, using the memory hole made it easier for the government to get people to engage in "duckspeak" (speaking without thinking), obviate "oldthink" (thoughts, beliefs or ideas enthused by past events, memories and history in the times before the revolution) and to encourage "blackwhite" (getting folks to believe that 2 + 2 is 5, or that white is black and black is white and to forget that one has ever believed anything different.

Over the past few years, a movement in the African American community has been afloat to remove all historical confederate reminders of the period in which the United States was engaged in a Civil War (1861-1865) and this scares me. Not because I support the confederacy or do not support the confederacy, but because I support history and learning and pedagogy. Removing these symbols will do nothing for black folk and make things a lot worse in my view. First, this is just cosmetic, it will not mean nothing, since when do you get your feeling hurt by looking at a flag or a statue of a many you don't know historically anything about? Robert E. Lee owned slaves sure, and he ran a plantation before the war, but he historically is no different than Thomas Jefferson or George Washington from this perspective. Are you upset with the state of Virginia too? Will it be next? After all Virginia was named after the person who introduced slavery to America. Half of the folk so offended likely couldn't tell you when the civil war was fought without the assistance of google nor have read any book about it or any other American wars for that fact.

I fear that without these historical reminders, being as lazy as we are with respect to reading and our penchant to watch TV more than we read, we will have forgot about this tragic and painful part of U.S. History and sleep walk back into a similar predicament in future generations. It isn't like we discuss history with our children anyway especially with this most recent generation. This is one reason why Marcus Garvey wrote "A people without the knowledge of their history, origin and culture is like a tree without roots."

Our incessant focus on memory holing history is idiotic and ridiculous. Why is it that we put more time into complaining about statues and flags than our kids killing each other on the streets of Chicago, Baltimore, New Orleans or Memphis every day? Why do we spend more energy on superficial actions when we can go around to any government public school and find more than half of the kids not proficient in ANY subject on grade level? Now these are worth attention, but nope, not sexy or dramatic enough (Deray trained yawl hypocrites well). I'm not offended or traumatized by any statute or flag. Why are we as black folk offended and traumatized by historical fact? Will removing them take the historical record away? Will it make more black folk richer? Will less of us live in poverty? Will we start more business? Will it lower STI rates in our community? NOPE – NOT ONE BIT. Because this is misdirected and misguided energy aimed at something that has no tangible impact on any black person in America unless you a puzzy with a soft as wet toilet paper mentally.

It seems as this fake synthetic outrage is becoming a contagious pandemic. Baltimore City Council has voted to remove four Confederate monuments in the city. Members of the Congressional Black Caucus want to remove all Confederate statues from the Capitol. Rep. Bennie Thompson (D-Miss.), told the Hill that "Confederate memorabilia have no place in this country and especially not in the United States

Capitol. These images symbolize a time of racial discrimination and segregation that continues to haunt this country and many African-Americans who still to this day face racism and bigotry." Can't make this up, so now black folks are afraid of ghost and haunted by images and symbols? Even more comedic is that magically, by removing these images and symbols, the past "time of racial discrimination and segregation" will either be forgotten or vaporize and end. Simple ain't it? Talk about historical revisionism and make-believe.

Bishop James Dukes, pastor of Liberation Christian Center, in Chicago is calling for the removal of a statue of statue George Washington and to have President Andrew Jackson's name removed from Washington and Jackson parks respectively, because they owned slaves. I suspect cats will be going after all confederate cemeteries and even the Confederate monuments in Gettysburg National Military Park (although Park and State officials say they will never be removed)

What will be next, removing all members of the confederacy or former slave owners from history books? Removing said history books from the libraries'? Preventing people from even writing books on the confederacy or slavery because "these images symbolize a time of racial discrimination and segregation that continues to haunt this country and many African-Americans who still to this day face racism and bigotry?" Will John C. Calhoun, a former vice president and staunch supporter of slavery be next? What about the Dallas Cowboy football team whose blue star is from the Bonnie Blue Flag (a banner of the Confederate States of America at the start of the American Civil War in 1861). Since many of us black folks do not read as much as previous generations, these two may be safe for as they say "to hide something from a nigg@, put it in a book."

Yes, one day our kids will not know anything about US history, slavery, the civil war or the deeds of many, good or bad, for the fear of as then Baltimore Mayor Stephanie Rawlings-Blake noted in signs that confederate monuments were just "part of a propaganda campaign" to "perpetuate the beliefs of white supremacy. "Again, although I am a black man, I will likely be called a racist piece of uninformed white trash, or worse – described as not being woke - for not supporting non-substantive cosmetic actions under the guise of African American self-determination and empowerment. But like the Taliban who destroyed the historical largest standing Buddha's, in the world in Bamiyan, who had been standing since the century, in Afghanistan, or ISIS, who destroyed the Temple of Baalshamin at the Syrian site of Palmyra because they found the offensive to Allah, similar suggestions about confederate monuments are equally claims of bull shit.

You do not have to agree with me but this is how I see it. If you do not believe me, just try to take down Auschwitz, Dachau or Buchenwald: Jews will never let it happen because they do not want anyone to forget about what happened to them so it will never happen again. Not us. They write and make documentaries incessantly on every aspect of the Holocaust and you will see at least one every day or weekly on TV around the world. Whether is on the Kristallnacht or the Nuremberg Laws or the Jews of Poland or the Jews of Lithuania or the human experimentation they tolerated, they telling their story. Not us, instead we get mad and formulate #Noconfederate because we too lazy to write and make our own and/or tell our own historical reality. Like I said. try to take down Auschwitz, Dachau or Buchenwald: Jews will never let it happen because they do not want anyone to forget about what happened to them so it will never happen again. Not us.

Much Ado About Kaepernick

I would like to preface this by saying first, please ignore any of the characteristics that some may consider privileged, such as being born in and living during segregation in Memphis in the early 1960s, my IQ of 165 plus, that I speak four languages and read a fifth, and teach statistics and neuroanatomy & behavior. With this out of the way – I don't give a grass hopper fck about Colin Kaepernick. I do care about him as a person, as I do all people, but I have no interest in his personal life or any other extraneous comportments regarding his existence and/or current circumstances. I have nothing against him and accept unconditionally that he is a Super bowl caliber quarterback with talents that exceed in my view, 85% of the current first, second and third string quarter backs in the NFL at this moment. However, being good at your job is only a portion of the job description.

Even with this, I do not understand why so many people are upset about him, one man, one man in the top 1 percent of income earners in the USA, not having a job, playing a game called football. Is it because of his afro (which I admit is cool)? Or is it because folks are in their feelings because he selected to take a knee during the national anthem in protest of something he clearly never believed in from the start and that he did for attention anyway? I can say this accurately, for after he noticed NFL owners not looking in his directions, he announced to the public via ESPN that next season he will stand during the under the simulacrum that he thinks his method of protest may be taking away from "positive change[s] he believes has been created."

If he were truthful, he would just admit that he is changing his tune because he misses that loot - them millions from being signed to a NFL team as a quarterback. Back-up quarterbacks make a nice little penny in the NFL. Which is another problem I have, why are folk so mad and want to protest on behalf of a single man? They do not protest about the many former NFL players (many of which are African Americans) suffering from Chronic Traumatic Encephalopathy (CTE) - the degenerative brain disease that is hypothesized to be the result of individuals suffering from repeated brain trauma. However, this would make too much sense, protesting for millions of dollars to go to research to understand the etiology and morphology surrounding how Tau proteins form, clumps and diffuse throughout the brain causing neural apoptosis in the process. The money that Kaepernick theoretically would be owed if under contract ($60 plus million) would go a long way for such research. But more than likely the people whom are upset that Kaepernick is unemployed may have Tau proteins of their own spreading throughout their brain given that C.T.E. often affects the pre frontal cortex, an area of the brain essential in executive function, cognition, working memory, planning and abstract reasoning and the amygdala which is important in emotional control, aggression and anxiety. Cleary these folks are not thinking and allowing emotion to overpower reason.

The truth is Kaepernick is far from broke and more important issues need to be in the forefront than him getting additional millions to by expensive sports cars. It is estimated that his net worth is between $16 and $22 million by some estimates. What I believe this is all about is the tendency for African Americans to be preoccupied by mindless self-absorbed celebrity twaddle (living vicariously through the lives of others). You make his problem your problem and develop a bond, albeit artificially concocted, of outrage rooted in thinking Colin is oppressed just like you – but he isn't. But in your maniacal (obsessive enthusiasm) psychosis (thought and emotions are so impaired that contact is lost with external reality), you create something that doesn't exist – he is being black balled. Maybe he is or maybe he isn't, regardless there is no evidence for either position, just conjecture.

There are several things that are being overlooked. The first is that the objective of any team, in this case a professional football is to win. Have anyone thought about what would happen if he was signed by a team. LeSean McCoy has and notes: "You just got to look at all sides, like if I'm an owner or the GM of a team, do I want to put him on my team? Is he good enough to be on the squad, to even deal with everything that's going on? That's something that I don't really partake in." Right or wrong, Kaepernick will be seen by some as a distraction not worth the attention. Then there is the fact that since his old coach left for the University of Michigan, he has not been the same performance wise.

So, people wake up. This is not important and please stop comparing this lickspittle to Muhammad Ali, who for the record never begged to get his job back or go to the media and say "I will go and fight the North Vietnamese and National Liberation Front, (Viet Cong) if you give me a job boxing again." Not to mention Ali was 100 percent African American, not that it matters, but Kaepernick is half white and was raised by a white couple who adopted him. We could be protesting many serious issues but unfortunately mindless celebrity twaddle wins again. Maybe we will realize our errors and protest Baltimore public schools where it was recently revealed that five Baltimore City high schools and one middle school do not have a single student proficient math and English, yet these schools have some of the highest graduation rates in the city. Or the senseless violence in our major urban and mostly black cities. But I doubt it, because the folks protesting a millionaire quarterback not having a job, likely went to public government schools.

The Growing Arrogance of Emmanuel Macron

After a few months, it appears that newly elected French President Emmanuel Macron is taking a page or two or three from the Donald Trump platform as well as Trump's display of vanity. Like a reincarnated but taller version of Napoleon, Macron paraded into the Palace of Versailles a while back announcing extensive new changes to the French political establishment. Macron has broadcast that he plans to reduce the number of delegates in both the upper and lower houses of parliament by a third which for lack of a better phrase is just one phase of him "draining the swamp." Macron has also channeled his Trumpian policy purview by focusing more and using tougher rhetoric. He is even pushing full steam ahead with his proposed tax cuts even given the $9.1 billion deficit in the French budget. However, the main observable overt behavioral comportment the new French president unfolds is a stuck-up and overbearing arrogance – even more than that of President Donald Trump.

He has other similarities to Trump also including his disdain for and continuous attempts to try and control the press. For example, he seldom speaks to the press and limits his public appearances to staged events in a similar manner as one of his unspoken political idols – Barack Obama. Like Trump, almost immediately after getting into office, he began to focus on fighting terrorism. First Macron created a counterterrorism task force. He has also increased spending on fighting terrorism in former French colonies in Africa. But for Macron, all of this is to make him look good and concentrate supreme power and authority, regardless if his actions have substance or not, in his hands alone.

All of this has led some to take note of Mr. Macron of "authoritarian" tendencies. In an interview, with Le Figaro he described his presidency and himself as the start of "a French renaissance [and] "European one as well," The 39-

year-old former Rothschild banker, has the support of the IMF and EU in his desire to decrease public spending. Then there are his proposed labor reforms, which has turned many of his voting block against him.   If people think that President Trump is arrogant and egotistical, then the same reasoning should fall in line for President Macron. Le Monde has reported that the president believes that his thinking did not "lend itself" to question and answer sessions such as those engendered during press conferences which resulted in him not having one on Bastille Day specifically because his"complex thoughts" may prove too much for journalists, reports say. Thus, in his mind, he Emmanuel Macron is too smart to communicate with, or to the serfs below him who put him in office. This may be why his popularity is even lower than the new U.S. President.

But if it were just smugness and disdain alone, he may not be perceived as so bad by the French populous. However, there are other things – policy, that adds to his pomposity. There are his views regarding France's labor code which he believes destroys jobs. Specifically, Macron's desire to harshly restrict payouts from labor boards to fired employees and reduce job protections. This singularly resulted in France's largest labor unions too take to the streets in protest. He has also cut social security allowances, housing subsidies, has proposed a partial lifting of the wealth tax and wishes to end local property taxes for 80 percent of those currently paying them starting in 2018. His actions with respect to politics in France are also being severel ridiculed because from afar (not including spending $30,000 on make-up), he appears to put the desires of the EU, like reducing the budget deficit to three percent than for what is best and wanted by the citizens of France. Budget Minister Gerald Darmanin recently announced that the macron administration would cut 13 billion euros in funding for towns, departments and regions by 2022 to meet the EU goals.

There is a growing group of government officials upset by the president. Some say he blames them when policies he has approved are observed as unpopular by the populace. Others feel that he (through his interior minister Gérard Collomb) ignored the needs of migrants when they refused to open a new reception center at Calais for them. Others opposition party members have gone on the record to describe Macron as having "absolutist tendencies." National Front Leader Marine Le Pen said that" the ruling party is "choosing its opposition."

Macron has guaranteed to change by decree (without any input or resistance from the French Parliament) to permanently make the antiterrorism state of emergency standard rule and to reduce the military budget by €850m which some believe led to the resignation of Pierre de Villiers, the head of the armed forces. His decision to address the Congress of the French Parliament ahead of the prime minister's policy statement was also viewed as condescending.

The Republicans accuse Macron's party of ignoring opposition when they appointed Thierry Solère of the majority, got an appointment (by secret ballot) that many say should have gone to the candidate of the largest opposition group, Republicans MP Eric Ciotti. Macron is also rubbing other European leaders the wrong way. Just this past week he questioned the EU's labor rules which allow firms to send temporary workers from low-wage countries to richer nations without having to pay social charges, causing Poland's foreign minister Witold Waszczykowski to suggest that the reason why Mr. Macron was attacking other nations was because the French economy under Macron was not as strong as Poland's economy.

Macron's ego has lead him to put civil security above liberty. Only Macron's Interior Ministry, with little review from the judicial branch has any say in searches and seizures and house arrests and the Macron administration can decide to close mosques if what is being said in them is not to their liking subjectively. Then there is way he talks about his populous as Italian psychiatrist Dr. Adriano Segator noted "When he talks about the poor or insults the workers of northern France, reducing them to smokers and alcoholics, when he denigrates women, lowering them to the level of the ignorant." But this only makes sense. From an economic perspective, he is the classic neoliberal. He wishes to want to lower corporatetaxes and the cost of labor and reduce the amount of regulations that he believes prevents French business from be competitive on the international stage. And like neoliberals in the US, Macron advances fiscal policy that place the needs of public interest and government privatization over the needs and rights of the people. If Macron isn't the perfect example of arrogance, no one is.

ABOUT THE AUTHOR

Torrance Stephens is originally from Memphis, Tennessee. He attended Morehouse College where he studied, psychology, biology and chemistry. He received a master's degree in Educational Psychology and Measurement from Atlanta University and a Ph.D. in Counseling from Clark Atlanta University. He has lived in Nigeria, Senegal, South Africa and several other African countries working with Africare International and conducting Infectious disease research. He is the author of several books including a novel, poems, essays and several collections of short prose. He was an Assistant Professor at Emory University in the Rollins School of Public Health in Atlanta for more than 14 years and until recently, as Associate Professor and Health Education/Health Promotion Track Coordinator for the MPH program at Morehouse School of Medicine in the Department of Community and Preventive Medicine. He is the father of two and currently lives in Palmetto, Georgia, and teaches Statistics at Clark Atlanta University in the Departments of Psychology and School of Education.